For Richard and Connie

Jim

Romanticism and American Architecture

Romanticism
and
American Architecture

James Early

New York: A.S. Barnes and Co., Inc.
London: Thomas Yoseloff Ltd

A.S. Barnes and Co., Inc.
8 East 36th Street
New York, N.Y. 10016

Thomas Yoseloff Ltd
18 Charing Cross Road
London W.C.2, England

6323

Printed in the United States of America

To the Memory of Perry Miller

Preface

With the current re-evaluation of Victorian culture has come an awakening to the fascinations of mid-nineteenth-century architecture, and a growing interest in its gems and follies, its Gothic revival churches and "Charles Addams" houses. Classical revival buildings have long been admired, but until recently, non-classical buildings have stood unnoticed, passed in the streets by eyes which did not see them. On the few occasions when they forced themselves into the modern esthetic consciousness, they were contemptuously dismissed as incoherent jumbles of forms constructed without any comprehensible system of design.

I have not cast myself as advocate for nineteenth-century architecture—it has notable and passionate champions both in Britain and America. My emphasis is upon the patterns of thought and feeling which fostered its development. This study of American architectural writings from the era of Thomas Jefferson to the time of Andrew Jackson Downing and Horatio Greenough is primarily concerned with the influence of Romantic ideas upon architectural thought and taste. Changing conceptions of history, of nature, of the nation, and of the work of art itself all affected the way men thought of architecture and what they saw when they looked at particular buildings. Romanticism produced a revolution in architecture probably greater than the one which divided the Renaissance from the Gothic period. I have attempted to discover the intellectual and emotional sources of the Romantic sense of form and to show how Romantic buildings are related to those of the preceding post-Renaissance tradition and to those of the twentieth century.

Although this book is limited to American architecture, many of its conclusions seem applicable to Romantic architecture generally. In an earlier form this study was a Harvard thesis in the History of American Civilization. I am indebted in many ways to the kindness and learning of Professors Benjamin Rowland and Perry Miller who directed it. I was most hospitably treated for a number of years by Miss Ruth V. Cook and Miss Edna Jones of the architectural library at Harvard. Professors Oscar Handlin, Charles Feidelson, Jr., and Vincent J. Scully, Jr., read the manuscript and suggested several ways of improving it. My other important debts are to Ann M. Early, to William R. Taylor and to Thomas J. McCormick.

Dallas, Texas
March, 1965

Table of Contents

Preface   7

Introduction: Jefferson's Capitol and the Older Classicism   13

1. The Romantic Revivals: History and Associationism   27

2. Romantic Naturalism: The Picturesque   51

3. Nature, the Gothic, and Functionalism   84

4. The Gothic as a Style for Protestantism   112

5. Nationalism and a New Architecture   137

Index   167

Romanticism and American Architecture

Introduction

Jefferson's Capitol and the Older Classicism

In September, 1785, Thomas Jefferson dispatched from Paris letters urging James Madison and Edmund Randolph to stop the construction of the Virginia capitol building. A few months earlier Jefferson had been asked to procure in Europe designs for that building, the governor's house, and a prison, all to be erected in Richmond, the recently established state capital. But to his mortification he learned that, without waiting for his plans, work was about to begin on a locally designed structure.

Madison and Randolph were able to stop the proceedings after the foundation had been laid for a bulky building with a portico on each of its four sides. Finally, in the following January, Jefferson was able to write to the Directors of the Public Building that he was sending plans based on the Maison Carrée at Nîmes. These had been drawn under his direction by Charles-Louis Clérisseau, who had studied and measured the Roman temple for his book, *Les Monuments de Nîmes*. Jefferson attempted to convince the directors that his structure would be economical, requiring but one portico and taking up only two-fifths of the area of the building which had been started. As for the foundation already in place, part could be retained and the bricks of the rest could be used for interior work. "Mortar never becomes so

13

hard and adhesive to the bricks in a few months but that it may easily be chipped off."

But Jefferson's main argument for his design was esthetic. He had wished for some time to introduce an example of the classical style of antiquity into Virginia,[1] and he assured the directors that the Maison Carrée "is allowed without contradiction to be the most perfect and precious remain of antiquity in existence . . . [superior to] anything at Rome, in Greece, at Balbec, or Palmyra."[2] Even from across the ocean Jefferson was persuasive, and Virginia's capitol became the first modern building modelled after a specific ancient edifice and the first example in the United States of the new type of classicism characteristic of the romantic movement.

Jefferson's strictures in the *Notes on Virginia* upon the "maledictions" of colonial architecture are well known. Much which he says seems unfair. He ignores the existence of domestic structures in stone or brick and harshly condemns those in wood. He writes of buildings weighted with "barbarous ornament" and finds almost nothing sufficiently chaste to suggest "the first principles of art." The intemperateness of his attack is best comprehended as the result of an innovator's impatience with the reigning taste. To understand his grievances against earlier American work, it is important to realize the nature of his architectural ideas and the ways in which they differ from those of his predecessors.

A comparison of Mount Airy of 1758, the most imposing of colonial Virginia houses, with the Richmond capitol will be useful in defining the radical quality of Jefferson's architecture. The symmetrical plan of Mount Airy, consisting of a rectangular main block connected to two subordinate structures by quadrantal passages, is common among British eighteenth-century country houses and derives ultimately from the sixteenth-century Italian architect, Andrea Palladio. Thomas T. Waterman traced the south front with its arcaded loggia to Plate LVIII of James Gibbs's *Book of Architecture*.[3] Many other features of the house were related by Waterman to the designs published in *Vitruvius Scoticus* by William Adam, a Scotch Palladian and father of the important architect, Robert Adam.[4]

Mount Airy is immediately recognizable as a structure intended for modern domestic use. It resembles no ancient model. Some of the ornamental features, notably the pediment and the loggia, are of antique inspiration but there is no columnar order on the south front. What is most impressive in the design is chiseled clarity and restraint. The classicism of Mount Airy is

Mount Airy, Richmond County, Virginia. (Photograph, H. B. Cook)

Capitol Richmond, Virginia. (Photograph, Wayne Andrews)

essentially a matter of spirit, consisting in a classical sense of order and repose rather than an imitation of specific classical forms.

In Jefferson's capitol a different point of view is apparent. Although the building reflects a sense of classical order, the primary emphasis is not upon classical qualities of design but upon the adaptation of a particular ancient temple form to modern purposes. Above all else Jefferson wished to create for the new center of government a recognizable copy of a specific historical monument. It is his insistence on literal imitation of the Maison Carrée, together with his sensitivity to the historical associations suggested by Roman structures, that characterizes Jefferson as an originator of romantic classicism.

The juxtaposition of the Richmond capitol and Mount Airy provides a convenient starting point in suggesting the nature of the change in classical architecture which accompanied the development of the romantic sensibility. But a brief consideration of the intellectual milieu in which structures like Mount Airy were created will contribute to a better understanding of the romantic architectural revolution. By the middle decades of the eighteenth century the more advanced American builders had come abreast of their English contemporaries stylistically. The mass of architectural books of the British Palladians of the circle of the Earl of Burlington and their followers provided colonial architects for the first time with a thorough knowledge of contemporary work in Britain. Houses such as Mount Airy were inspired by plates found in British books. Even the designs of Peter Harrison, the most distinguished architect in the American colonies, were dependent upon his extensive library. Only the last and most modest of Harrison's works, Christ Church in Cambridge, is not closely derived from the plates of British Palladians, such as William Kent and Colin Campbell, or from Edward Hoppus's edition of Palladio's works.

Country houses like Mount Airy and their British prototypes are characteristic products of the earlier eighteenth century and are related in spirit to both literary classicism and the scientific movement of Descartes and Newton. The architectural theories of the Burlington group, like the *Discourses on Art* of Sir Joshua Reynolds, are based upon general principles considered applicable in all circumstances. Men of the time sought in the classical past not what was specifically Roman or Greek but what was universally appealing beyond any temporary shift in fashion. The belief in a uniform standard of taste valid for all arts in all ages is analogous to Newton's effort to comprehend all the diversity of the physical universe within a single system of mathematical laws.

The objectivity, sobriety, and logic of Palladian architecture is related to the "close, naked, natural way of speaking . . . near [to] . . . mathematical plainness" advocated by the scientists of the Royal Academy [5] and to the neo-classical abhorrence of subjective extravagance in literature. The relation between Palladian buildings and specific Roman monuments seems akin to the doctrine of idealized imitation derived by men of letters from Aristotle's *Poetics* [6] and to the generalizing cast of mind fostered by mathematically oriented science.

Another work at least as influential as *The Poetics* or Newton's *Principia Mathematica* in creating habits of thought congenial to English Palladianism was Locke's *Essay Concerning Human Understanding*. Locke held that there are no innate ideas, that all our ideas are based ultimately upon sense experience. Eighteenth-century architects and estheticians, starting from this conception of the mind, reasoned that if ideas were dependent upon sensation, architecture must be clearly organized in order to produce strong and sharply defined sensations.[7] The Lockean stress upon sense impressions fused with the Palladian admiration for the strong and ordered architecture of Rome.

Mount Airy and similar creations of post-Renaissance classicism were not particularly intended to recall the Roman past. Instead they exemplify the application to modern needs of general principles of design derived from ancient architecture. The sharply defined order of the plan and façade of Mount Airy reflects such Vitruvian prescriptions for architecture as symmetry, propriety, and eurythmy. These classical characteristics are in complete accord with a taste shaped by the psychology of Locke and the world scheme of Newton. Mount Airy's orderly relation of parts answers the Lockean demand for simple esthetic images and its rational sobriety harmonizes with the ideals of the New Science.

Unlike the earlier classicists, Jefferson's primary concern was not with the general principles of design conceived to be responsible for the timeless appeal of classical buildings. Although Jefferson, like the Palladians, emphasized the universal appeal of Roman architecture, arguing that the beauty of the Maison Carrée was insured by almost two thousand years and the suffrage of the entire world, he placed great importance on preserving the exact proportions of the ancient temple. He recommended that the directors restore the third row of columns of the Maison Carrée which Clérisseau had omitted from the plans in order to secure more light for the interior and save money. Jefferson feared that any tampering with the ancient design might destroy its charm. His insistence on the value of a close copy gives the capitol its

Maison Carrée, Nîmes. (Photograph, Alexander Frenkley)

Parlor of Oak Hill, Peabody, Mass., by Samuel McIntire.
(Photograph courtesy of Museum of Fine Arts, Boston)

great importance in architectural history. It sets it off from the generalizing classicism of Jefferson's Palladian predecessors and links it to the growing historical-mindedness of the Romantic movement. Architectural classicism was to be increasingly influenced by the particularity of history rather than the generality of the natural sciences.

Although Jefferson's Richmond capitol had preceded by twenty years comparable European adaptations of classical buildings for modern use, most American architects at the end of the century were conservative followers of the English Palladian or French academic traditions. The principal innovation was the attenuated manner of Robert Adam which influenced architects such as the New Englanders Charles Bulfinch and Samuel McIntire. Asher Benjamin's *The Country Builder's Assistant*, the first American architectural book, made Adamesque details available to a generation of carpenter-architects.

As there was no clear break with the architecture of colonial times, neither was there any fundamental shift from the patterns of ideas which had supported this architecture. Lockean and Newtonian thinking remained dominant in the United States in the years following the establishment of the new government. The newest philosophical importation, Scotch-Realism, merely reinterpreted Locke's epistemology to protect it from the assault of David Hume.

When the architectural revolution foreshadowed by the Richmond capitol finally took place, the archeologically inspired classical revivals were nourished and shaped by the same patterns of thought which had supported the earlier classicism. This is exemplified in the buildings and writings of Benjamin Henry Latrobe, a versatile and restless Englishman who was the most important initiator of the Greek revival in the United States. Latrobe worked in Virginia, Philadelphia, Baltimore, Washington, and New Orleans, training promising young men like Robert Mills and William Strickland, and establishing architecture as a profession in this country. He conceived of Greek architecture primarily as an architecture of simplicity and clarity and he saw Greek revivalism as part of a general movement towards simplicity in the arts and in manners. His criticism of a notorious architectural fiasco, the house of Robert Morris in Philadelphia, reflects the influence of Lockean psychology. He wrote that the horizontal and perpendicular lines were broken up so that "the whole mass altogether gives no idea at first sight to the mind sufficiently distinct to leave an impression." [8]

House of Robert Morris, Philadelphia, Pierre Charles L'Enfant. Watercolor by Thomas or William Birch. (Courtesy of the Library Company of Philadelphia)

City Hall, New York. Aquatint. (Courtesy of the Museum of the City of New York)

Second Bank of the United States, Philadelphia.
(Photograph, Antonelli School of Photography)

Classical revivalists soon went beyond their Palladian predecessors in quest of the architectural simplicity which they believed could alone be adequately grasped by the mind. Increasingly the massing of post-Renaissance classical structures seemed cluttered and the detail fussy, until only the simple clarity of archeologically pure antique forms seemed completely satisfactory. And before long even the buildings of Roman classicism appeared confusing and lacking in the simple grandeur of the Greek. Indicative of rapidly shifting taste in the 1820's is the beginning of the reaction against prominent public buildings designed in the older manner. The change is well illustrated by the critical fortune of the New York City Hall of 1803, one of the finest post-Renaissance buildings in this country. Its traditional ground plan of projecting end pavilions and receding central block made it seem in 1827 to a writer in the *Philadelphia Monthly Magazine* diffuse and without sufficient force. He maintained that the larger portion of the mass should have been placed in the foreground to catch the sunlight, and that only confusion results from dividing a large mass "by parts in alternate advances and retreats." [9] For another advocate of antique simplicity the façade seemed "deformed with a mass of gingerbread work." [10] The critic in the *Philadelphia Monthly Magazine* contrasted with the New York City Hall the handling of the mass in William Strickland's Second Bank of the United States in Philadelphia, a structure patterned on the Parthenon. There, he felt, the spectator "is forcibly struck with the grand impressive appearance of the front . . . [because of] the unity and *entireness of view* under which it is presented to him. The platform with its gradation of steps, the massive yet well-proportioned columns, the long line of entablature, and surmounting pediment, are embraced by the eye at the first glance." [11]

NOTES

1. Marie Kimball, *Jefferson: The Scene of Europe 1784 to 1789* (New York: Coward-McCann, 1950), 71.

2. Letter to William Buchanan and James Hay, *The Papers of Thomas Jefferson* (Princeton: Princeton University Press, 1954). IX, 220–222.

3. *The Mansions of Virginia* (Chapel Hill: University of North Carolina Press, 1946), 256.

4. *Ibid.*, 156, 259.

5. Thomas Sprat, *History of the Royal Society* (London, 1667), 112.

6. More completely than any architectural writing of the period the *Discourses on Art* of Sir Joshua Reynolds show how classicism in the visual arts paralleled the classical

theories of literature which descended from Aristotle. For Reynolds, idealized imitation was the proper method for the young painter. He conceded that nature is the ultimate basis of beauty of form but scorned the "mere copiers of nature [who] can never produce anything great; can never raise and enlarge the conceptions or warm the heart of the spectator." For insight into the true simplicity of nature he advised thorough study of the old masters. After relating art to nature and to the great works of the past, Reynolds went on to stress the value of the general idea which alone constitutes real excellence in art. Beauty for him was general and intellectual; it resulted from the assimilation of classical principles rather than imitation of particular classical works. *Longinus on the Sublime and Reynolds Discourses on Art* (Chicago: Packard, 1945), 117, 125, 132, 172. See also the most theoretical of English Palladian architectural books, Isaac Ware's *A Complete Body of Architecture* (London, 1756) Cf. (2nd ed.; London, 1768), 134, 482.

7. Cf. Ware *op. cit.*, 296; Sir William Chambers, *A Treatise on Civil Architecture* (London, 1759), 18; Reynolds in *op. cit.*, 148, 149, 169–170, 201, 212.

8. *The Journal of Latrobe* (New York, 1905), 91–92.

9. "The Arts and Artists," *Philadelphia Monthly Magazine*, vol. I, no. 1 (1827), 17.

10. "City Improvements," *New York Mirror*, vol. XII, no. 8, 57.

11. "The Arts and Artists," *loc. cit.*, 17.

I

The Romantic Revivals:
History and Associationism

ARRIVING IN NEW YORK BY WAY OF THE EAST RIVER IN THE SPRING OF 1831, Alexis de Tocqueville was delighted by "a number of little palaces of white marble, several of which were of classic architecture." His enthusiasm was dampened when he learned, upon closer inspection the following day, that the "marble temples" had walls of whitewashed brick and columns of painted wood. In the deception De Tocqueville found evidence of the "hypocrisy of luxury," a vice he believed inherent in democracies where "appearance is more attended to than reality." [1] A century and a quarter later such architectural masquerading seems more characteristic of the romantic age than of democratic societies. Showiness was almost inevitable in a period that characteristically valued the aura of nostalgic associations surrounding particular architectural forms more than the forms themselves. All the romantic revivals, both classical and medieval, were marked by some degree of theatricality. Nicholas Biddle's remodelling of his country house, Andalusia, by tacking on a portico modelled on the Athenian Hephaisteron seems only somewhat less theatrical than Edwin Forrest's staging a great quasi-medieval entertainment for the workers to celebrate the "roofing" of Fonthill Castle, his battlemented house above the Hudson at Riverdale. The flamboyance of romantic architecture contributed to its appeal. Buildings imbued with nostalgic recollections of centuries gone by and associated with exotic and almost forgotten

Andalusia, Andalusia Pa. (Photograph, Wayne Andrews)

Fonthill Castle, Riverdale, New York. (Photograph, Wayne Andrews)

customs struck the imaginations of restive members of an overwhelmingly middle-class society. Greek churches and Gothic houses relieved the monotonous newness of American cities and provided a vicarious sense of history for the recently cleared countryside.

In diverse ways the growth of romantic revivalism seems related to the broadening of American democracy in the first half of the nineteenth century. During this period politics became much more democratic and many of the old social barriers became less important. Romantic structures appealed to those who lamented the disappearance of aristocratic distinctions of manner and sought to be apart from the crowd. Baronial country houses in the Hudson Valley and Greek mansions in the Philadelphia area and the Mississippi Delta provided an aura of aristocracy for the newly rich of the theatre, the financial community, and the plantation, and gave assurance to the socially insecure. In contrast to its appealing to aristocratic longings within an increasingly democratic society, revivalist architecture seems related also to the democratic emphasis upon the equality of individuals. Previously artists and craftsmen had been accustomed to work within a broadly accepted style which was sanctioned by cultivated taste and craft tradition. The anarchic eclecticism of romantic architecture is in keeping with the new stress upon egalitarian individualism. For the first time there was no single dominant style and an almost complete freedom of choice was possible for the architect or the patron. The older sense of a cultural community under the influence of a refined minority was sacrificed to the democratic belief in the taste of every man.

The full pageantry of high romantic eclecticism did not become prevalent until the eighteen-thirties and, to some degree, as we have seen, revival buildings, both classical and medieval,[2] reflected patterns of thought inherited from the previous century. But many characteristics of this architecture stem from newer romantic conceptions which were often antithetical to the older assumptions. Emotion and sentiment were often more important than logic and rationality in shaping the growth of the revivals. The desire to imitate in modern times for modern purposes the buildings of the past is ultimately incomprehensible without an understanding of peculiarly romantic habits of thought and feeling. Provincial American imitations of the Parthenon and King's College Chapel are alike difficult to account for apart from the romantic longing for the old, the distant, and the emotionally exciting.

Before passing to mature romanticism, consider the architectural effect of the proto-romantic fascination with the sublime. This conception originated in the antique treatise attributed to Longinus and seemed at first to support classical architecture. Only later were its full anti-classical implications understood. Edmund Burke, whose *Inquiry into the Origin of our Ideas of the Sublime and Beautiful* was the most influential English work on the sublime, credited classical temples with sublimity because of an effect of artificial infinity created by the succession and uniformity of their parts which led the spectator to believe that they extended beyond their actual limits. They derive grandeur from giving the eye no boundaries to settle upon and thus denying the imagination any rest.[3] In the United States a view of classical architecture analogous to Burke's was common. Jefferson described the designs based on the Maison Carrée he sent to Virginia as "simple and sublime." [4] The novelist, Cooper, wrote that on entering the Pantheon the spectator is "struck by its simple and beautiful grandeur," that the effect of the great interior is to enlist the sense of sight "on the side of omnipotence, infinite majesty, and perfect beauty." [5] The idea of the sublime lies behind much American classical revival architecture. It explains in part the continuing appeal of this architecture for an age influenced by romantic ideas.

While the theory of the sublime was first used architecturally to explain the appeal of classical buildings, before long it was seen that the theory of the sublime could be applied just as well to non-classical architectural styles. Early eighteenth-century critics like Addison felt that the small scale of Gothic ornament prevented the style from being sublime.[6] But once the underlying unity of vertical direction was appreciated, the esthetic impact of the style was felt. "The eye sees much, but so closely and intimately connected, that the mind is occupied only with the idea of one grand whole." [7] Eventually the Gothic came to seem far more sublime than classical architecture which, consequently, lost favor.

Of greater architectural consequence than the cult of the sublime was the tremendous growth of interest in history characteristic of the romantic movement. Historians of the Enlightenment had assumed human nature to be unchanging, and conveniently ignoring, as the Dark Ages, periods in which men behaved differently from themselves, they had concentrated on recent history and on congenial periods of ancient history. The romantic movement abandoned the universalizing tendency of the Enlightenment and valued diversity for its own sake. Typical of this interest in diversity was the new view of history. Instead of reading their own ideas and interests back into history in the belief that they were natural to men of all ages, the romanticists valued the distinctness of other cultures and epochs; they thought it important

The Pantheon, Rome. Painting by Giovanni Paolo Panini.
(National Gallery of Art, Washington, D.C., Samuel H. Kress Collection)

The Old House of Representatives. Painting by Samuel F. B. Morse
in the Collection of the Corcoran Gallery of Art.

to try to understand alien civilizations through an imaginative projection of
the self. For the romanticists the classical past which had been, as it were,
lifted from the stream of time by the Enlightenment, became a historical
period to be studied like other historical periods. Now its appeal largely consisted in its antiquity rather than in its timelessness.

With the growing historical consciousness came the new science of archeology. Architects since Brunelleschi had been interested in the remains of
the Roman past, and Englishmen had collected Greek vases and inscriptions
since the time of James I, but archeology became of great importance only
in the mid-eighteenth century with the appearance of the Comte de Caylus'
Recueil d'Antiquités Egyptiennes, Etrusques, Greques et Romaines in 1752
and the publication in 1754 of the discoveries at Herculaneum and Pompeii
which had been excavated by Charles VII of Naples. The Society of Dilet-
tanti, founded in England, aided in the study of classical archeology and
made possible the publication of such works as Stuart and Revett's *Antiquities of Athens*, Richard Chandler's *Ionian Antiquities*, Robert Wood's *Ruins
of Palmyra* and *Ruins of Balbec*, and Robert Adam's *Ruins of the Palace of
the Emperor Diocletian at Spalatro*. Such studies provided accurate measured
drawings which proved to be of great use to historically minded architects
who, instead of abstracting from classical precedent like the earlier classicists,
copied the columnar orders from famous classical buildings. The *Antiquities
of Athens* was indispensable to the architects of the Greek Revival in
America, most of whom never saw a Greek building. Archeological books
which made possible accuracy in reproducing the architecture of particular
historical periods were in tune with the new romantic desire to understand
the diverse forms of human nature manifested in the course of history. By
the beginning of the nineteenth century archeologists were at work with
medieval and Egyptian antiquities. Their work in both fields was utilized
by architects in succeeding decades.

In esthetics as well as in history profound changes in outlook appeared
with the coming of romanticism. One of the most significant British works
of the early romantic movement is Archibald Alison's *Essays on the Nature
and Principles of Taste*, which was published in 1790. The associationism of
Alison and his followers was extremely influential both in England and in
the United States, and apart from its direct influence, it represents a characteristic romantic attitude towards art which must be understood by students of revivalist architecture. Alison undermined the basis of the conception
of abstract beauty which was central to Renaissance classicism; he denied that

any forms whatever are beautiful in themselves [8] and maintained that they seem beautiful (or sublime) only because of the thoughts which they raise in the mind of the spectator. In considering the claim of particular proportions to abstract beauty, he held that in purely utilitarian structures beauty of the walls consists merely in fitness for stability and support. He admitted that mere fitness to support an entablature does not explain the appeal of the classical orders but argued that that was due, not to their following of certain abstract proportions, but to extraneous things such as their ornamentation, the skill of their execution, and the elegant purposes which they serve; in short, their appeal is based on extrinsic associations. Alison went on to say that "there are other Associations we have with these forms, that still more powerfully serve to command our admiration; for they are the GRECIAN orders; they derive their origin from those times, and were the ornament of those countries which are most hallowed in our imaginations; and it is difficult for us to see them, even in their modern copies, without feeling them operate upon our minds, as relics of those polished nations where they first arose, and of that greater people by whom they were afterwards borrowed." [9] Later Alison attributed the beauty of Gothic revival forms to the fact that they lead "to ideas of Gothic manners and adventure." [10]

The denial that there was anything particularly beautiful about architectural forms in themselves constituted a break with the whole tradition of Renaissance and post-Renaissance architectural theory. Palladio and his predecessors believed that certain forms and proportions were beautiful because they accorded with the basic harmony of the universe; the eighteenth-century Palladians, who commonly rejected that neo-Platonic doctrine, still maintained that the forms of classical architecture were abstractly beautiful. Beauty for this whole tradition was objective; before the Romantic Period all agreed that beauty inhered in the forms themselves, not in the subjective reaction of the mind of the spectator. Alison's stress on the importance of historical associations for the appreciation of classical and Gothic architecture significantly fuses the developing romantic interest in history with the new subjectivism in esthetics. The combination of historical-mindedness and this new subjectivism was of immense importance in nineteenth-century revivalist architecture.

No American wrote an esthetic treatise comparable to Alison's or to Richard Payne Knight's *Analytical Inquiry into the Principles of Taste*,[11] but American architectural theorists showed their debt to the associationists. Asher Benjamin and Minard Lafever, who with Andrew Jackson Downing were the most prolific and influential writers of architectural books in the first half of the nineteenth century in the United States, both read Alison and propagated his theory.[12] The associationist approach to architecture was pervasive among thousands who had never heard of Alison. Emotional response to the historical suggestiveness of revivalist structures was general in the Romantic Period. Alison merely systematized something which was characteristic of the romantic sensibility. Philip Hone, for example, auctioneer and Mayor of New York, recorded in his diary his reaction to the classic forms of a seaside hotel he owned at Rockaway. When the moon was setting over the neighboring hills, Hone wrote, "the lofty columns of the noble piazza, breaking the silver streams into dark and gloomy shadows, gave the edifice the appearance of some relic of classic antiquity." [13] Such historical reveries stimulated by revivalist architecture constituted an important element of its appeal. Much of the attraction of classical architecture had since the Renaissance been due to its connection with the admired Roman past, but in the nineteenth century the dependence upon historical associations became extreme.

The obverse of the romantic interest in architectural styles richly suggestive of the past was a neglect of architecture which lacked such suggestions. Renaissance architecture, which was of a past too recent to provide sentimental reveries, lost general favor during most of the early nineteenth century. James Jackson Jarves, the first important American collector of early Italian paintings, was typical in deprecating Renaissance architecture because it "arouses no emotion beyond intellectual approbation of the purity of its materials, the beauty of its proportions, and the high finish of its ornament." [14] Mrs. Nathaniel Hawthorne's comments on the Medici-Riccardi Palace are revealing. She wrote reproachfully that this mid-fifteenth-century structure "has an ever-enduring newness of aspect" so that "no ruin can ever be imagined of it." The Florentine Renaissance palaces seemed timeless to her and this she held against them. "They can never decay, and never appear old. . . . When I look at those dark, indestructible, gloomy palaces, they terrify me with a sense of hopelessness. They are defiant with strength, and like prisons from which there is no escape. But always they seemed to be finished to-day, and not belong to the past." An architecture which "seemed to be finished to-day" was far less appealing to the romantic sensibility than one that was clearly connected with the distant past. Mrs. Hawthorne had as much enthusiasm for the Colosseum as she had disdain for the Medici-Riccardi Palace. She delighted in its signs of age, and dwelt on the age-

The Medici-Riccardi Palace, Florence. (Photograph, Alinari)

The Colosseum. Etching by Giovanni Battista Piranesi.

softened color of its stone. She thought that it looked "hoary with the years that have passed" and called it "the Ruin of Ruins." [15]

The fascination with ruins, which colored Mrs. Hawthorne's attitude towards the Colosseum as late as 1858, was a feature of the romantic mentality from the beginning. Fiske Kimball has shown that romantic revivalism in architecture, both classical and medieval, appeared first in ornaments in the gardens of eighteenth-century England along with artificial ruins.[16] In both the Roman and Gothic styles the erection of sham ruins seems to have preceded the imitation of whole buildings.[17] In any case, the erection of ruins and of imitations of whole buildings in past styles both seem motivated by a similar desire to promote reveries concerning the past. More exotic structures which were built in the romantic English gardens included Egyptian obelisks, Chinese pagodas, and Mohammedan mosques. Oddly enough, some of the men who were most soberly Palladian in their serious architecture were leaders in designing romantic garden edifices. Lord Burlington, himself, built a watch charm Pantheon for the gardens at Chiswick, and his protégé, William Kent, constructed a tiny Roman temple with a free-standing colonnade. Sir William Chambers designed a series of garden structures for the gardens at Kew which included classic temples, a ruined triumphal arch, a Gothic church, a House of Confucius and a pseudo-Moorish "Alhambra."

In the United States, Jefferson hoped to have a romantic garden at Monticello with specimens of Gothic and Chinese architecture as well as models of the Pantheon and cubic architecture. As early as 1771, in planning a temple over a spring, he wrote that "the roof may be Chinese, Grecian, or in the taste of the Lantern of Demosthenes at Athens." In the same year Jefferson jotted down some notes on a burying place; he planned to erect "a small Gothic temple of antique appearance" in the center of a circular area in an unfrequented part of the park surrounded by aged oaks and gloomy evergreens where there is "no sound to break the stillness but a brook, that bubbling winds among the weeds; no mark of any human shape that had been there, unless the skeleton of some poor wretch, who sought that place out to despair and die in." [18] These entries in his *Pocket Account Book* clearly show that Jefferson more than a decade before he visited Europe or designed the first structure of the classical revival in America had assimilated the characteristic eighteenth-century romantic attitude towards nature and death and towards architectural forms which recalled old times and distant places. The fascination with death and the dying, so notable in writers like Irving and Poe, was to contribute to the popularity of medieval and, especially, Egyptian architecture.

Full scale structures in the Gothic and other styles which seemed exotic began to appear with increasing frequency as romantic eclecticism of taste moved outside the garden walls and invaded the province of serious architecture. Jefferson was unique among the important revivalist architects of the United States in limiting himself to classical styles. Latrobe, who introduced Greek forms into the United States, built the first Gothic country house in America, Sedgely. For the Catholic Cathedral of Baltimore, he provided both Gothic and classical designs and wrote that he had "an equal desire to see the first or the second erected" because his habits inclined him towards the second and his reason preferred the first.[19] Latrobe later designed two other Gothic churches, a masonry-vaulted Gothic bank, and an Egyptian scheme for the Congressional library. More conservative architects like Charles Bulfinch, Josiah Brady, and John Holden Greene also worked in the Gothic idiom, as did men who were primarily Greek revivalists such as William Strickland, Ithiel Town, Isaiah Rogers, Solomon Willard, and Minard Lafever. John Haviland designed, in addition to Greek and Gothic buildings, the Tombs Prison in New York in the Egyptian style. Strickland and Thomas U. Walter also did Egyptian work. Richard Upjohn used the Greek, Gothic, Romanesque and Italian villa styles. In 1867 the great eclectic, Alexander Jackson Davis, listed in his diary fourteen different styles he used for suburban and country houses; among the styles were Collegiate Gothic, "Switz" cottage, Lombard Italian, Tuscan from Pliny's villa at Ostia, Ancient Etruscan, Suburban Greek, Oriental, and Moorish.[20]

Although the romantic sensibility was receptive to a rich variety of architectures, for many years the classical styles were much more popular than the Gothic or more exotic modes. The Greek revival came close to becoming the national style in the United States in the eighteen-thirties and forties. Andrew Jackson, James K. Polk, and Robert E. Lee all lived in Greek revival houses. The fashion swept official Washington and Greek custom houses, banks, and hotels came to dominate the principal cities. At least a dozen state capitols were Grecian, ranging from Connecticut to California and most numerous in the new states of the Mississippi Valley. Meanwhile the revived Gothic made much slower progress in the United States than in England. One thing which inhibited American adoption was the continuing influence of eighteenth-century ideas which put a premium on order, clarity, and simplicity, qualities more characteristic of classical than of Gothic style. Then, too, the plainness of classical architecture appealed to the sober morality of a predominantly middle class Protestant people. In church design

The Architects Dream, painting by Thomas Cole,
The Toledo Museum of Art, gift of Florence Scott Libby, 1949.

Andrew Jackson's home, The Hermitage, near Nashville.
(Photograph by Paul A. Moore, Tennessee Conservation Department)

the lingering influence of what Anthony Garvan has called the Protestant Plain Style delayed the medieval phase of romantic revivalism. Gothic has, since its revival, been preeminently an ecclesiastical style, and to many it seemed too sensuous and frivolous for Protestant worship.[21]

Yet the immense popularity of classical architecture and the relative neglect for many years of Gothic in the United States are not entirely explicable by reference to Protestant asceticism and to the continuing influence of the older ideas. Certain conditions unique to the United States caused the developing romantic sensibility to work initially on behalf of romantic classicism and to neglect the Medieval styles. In a country without a Medieval past and where higher education consisted largely in a reading of classical authors, the influence of the growing interest in history was directed almost exclusively in support of classical architecture. Gothic structures seemed alien to the national tradition, to reek of the dark ages of European despotism and the superstitions of Catholicism. Only after Scott popularized the Middle Ages could Medieval architecture compete with classical as a stimulus to the romantic imagination in America.

If the Middle Ages seemed foreign and hostile, educated Americans of the first romantic generation liked to connect their republic with the republics of the ancient world and often tried rather self-consciously to pattern their lives after the ancients. Jefferson's construction of a house on a mountaintop was at the same time a remarkable manifestation of the new romantic attitude towards nature and a desire to emulate his beloved Romans; Monticello was given certain features typical of the hillside villas occupied by such Romans as Cicero, Varro, and Pliny.[22]

The tendency of Americans to associate their new government with the free republics of antiquity led to the use of classical architecture for public buildings. Jefferson expressed to Latrobe the hope that the new capitol in Washington would be an honorable monument of the young republic, worthy of comparison with the remains of the classical republics, decorating with Athenian taste a nation aspiring to more than Athenian destinies.[23] The extent to which Americans of the early nineteenth century associated ancient Greece and its architecture with their new republic is revealed by things such as Fenimore Cooper's description of George Washington as having a character that "was Doric, in all its proportions." [24]

The architectural descriptions of travelers in Europe during this period bring out the vividness of the classical past for the American imagination. Although Medieval architecture is almost never related to the period of its

George Washington, by Horatio Greenough. National Collection of Fine Arts,
Smithsonian Institution, Washington, D.C.

construction by travelers, classical buildings are very frequently imagined existing in the midst of life in antique times. Jefferson in viewing the Roman remains in southern France was inspired with thoughts of the classical past. "From a correspondent at Nîmes," he wrote in 1787 to the Comtesse de Tessé, "you will not expect news. Were I to attempt to give you news, I should tell you stories one thousand years old. I should detail to you the intrigues of the courts of the Caesars, how they affect us here, the oppressions of their praetors, prefects, etc. I am immersed in antiquities from morning to night. For me the city of Rome is actually existing in all the splendor of its empire." [25]

After examining the climate of taste and ideas which supported the revivals, it is well to consider the quality of revivalist architecture. One persistent question concerns propriety. Historically modelled edifices seem well enough suited for certain monumental purposes, but for many other modern needs revivalist structures are grotesquely inappropriate. In the United States the popular Greek revival style was often adopted in situations where it was clearly unsuitable. Lack of restraint in its application provoked a rational reaction against the style, and it provided plenty of ammunition for those who preferred Gothic or Renaissance architecture.

"An extraordinary taste is afflicting this country in the way of architecture," remarked a character in Cooper's *Home as Found* of 1838, "nothing but a Grecian temple being now deemed a suitable residence for a man in these classical times." His companion replied that "one such temple well placed in a wood, might be a pleasant object enough; but to see a river lined with them, with children trundling hoops before their doors, beef carried into their kitchens, and smoke issuing, moreover, from those unclassical objects, is too much ever for a high taste." He went on to say that he had been told of "one town in the interior that has actually a market-house on the plan of the Parthenon." [26] Four years later Andrew Jackson Downing wrote that "it would certainly be difficult for a stranger in some of our towns, where the taste for Grecian temples prevails, to distinguish with accuracy between a church, a bank, and a hall of justice." [27]

The absence of an established architectural profession contributed to this widespread use in the United States of the classical temple form for all kinds of buildings. In Europe where professional architects exerted a substantial influence, extreme revivalism was kept in relative check. Amateurs were generally more susceptible to the associational appeal of revival architecture,[28] and amateurs like Jefferson, Napoleon, Catherine of Russia, and

Ludwig I of Bavaria played important roles in pushing the revival to an extreme imitation of classical buildings. In France, where the architectural profession was powerful, the academic tradition did not succumb to revivalism and classicism was confined, despite the influence of Napoleon, to monuments and to a few public buildings.

Other amateurs besides Jefferson furthered the revivalist movement in the United States. Latrobe, designer of the Bank of Pennsylvania, gave credit to Samuel M. Fox, president of that bank, "for the existence and taste." [29] of this building with Ionic porticoes copied from Stuart and Revett's plate of the north porch of the Erectheum. Nicholas Biddle, one of the few Americans to visit Greece in the early nineteenth century, was an influential advocate of Greek revival architecture. Talbot Hamlin attributed to his influence the precedence of Philadelphia over other American cities in the use of Greek forms.[30] Biddle saw to it that the terms of the competition for the design of the Second Bank of the United States expressed a preference for the temple shape. He convinced Thomas U. Walter of the desirability of abandoning his own prize-winning design for Girard College in favor of a structure enveloped in a Corinthian colonnade.[31]

In comparison with these amateurs, professional architects were more aware of the functional necessities in modern buildings and, on the whole, were less impressed by associational values. The architectural functionalism which originated among eighteenth-century neo-classical theoreticians in Europe is well exemplified in the school of Latrobe.

The difference between the amateur's indiscriminate love of antique forms and the professional's rationalistic respect for modern functional necessities is epitomized by an exchange of letters between Jefferson and the architect of the national Capitol. Jefferson wrote to Latrobe objecting to a cupola designed for the top of the central dome of the building, remarking that he had never seen such a form used in classical structures and considered cupolas ugly. He went on to suggest that the dome be modelled on the Roman Pantheon.[32]

Latrobe's rationalist respect for function in architectural design is revealed in his reply. He conceded that cupolas were not particularly handsome and stated: when "the Grecian style can be copied without impropriety, I love to be a mere, I would say a *slavish*, copyist, but the forms and the distribution of the Roman and Greek buildings which remain are in general inapplicable to the objects and uses of our public buildings. Our religion requires churches wholly different from the temples, our government, our legislative assemblies, and our courts of justice, buildings of entirely different principles from their basilicas; and our amusements could not possibly be performed in their theatres or amphitheatres. But that which principally demands a variation in our buildings from those of the ancients is the difference of our climate." As to the subject under discussion, Latrobe went on, "I cannot admit that because the Greeks and Romans did not place elevated cupolas upon their temples, they may not when necessary be rendered also beautiful." The question as to a cupola's being in good taste depends upon its utility because nothing "can be beautiful which appears useless or unmeaning. If our climate were such as to admit of doing legislative business in open air, that is under the light of an open orifice in the crown of a dome as at the Parthenon [sic], I would never put a cupola on any spherical dome. It is not the *ornamental*, it is the use that I want." [33]

During the period of romantic revivalism the creative spirit of the best architects was frustrated all too often; the architectural profession was new in the United States and the influence of the amateur dominated; time and again the more original architects had to submit to the popular view which saw buildings in terms of associational values. Walter submitted to the taste of Biddle in the work he did at Girard College and at Biddle's home, Andalusia. Both William Strickland and Latrobe were willing to squeeze the functions of a modern bank [34] into the Doric temple form admired by Biddle.

If the popular romantic esthetic led to irrationally literal adaptations of classical structures for modern use, it also led to a loss of refinement in architectural design. Revivalist architecture originated in structures erected in gardens in order to evoke in visitors a mood of romantic nostalgia for the past. Obviously the associations to be suggested were the principal concern in the design of these edifices. The specifically architectural quality of such structures was relatively unimportant. The associational approach to architectural form continued to influence revivalist architecture long after it left the garden world of its creation. The American countryside abounds in carpenter-built versions of classical and Gothic designs which, though sometimes charming, have less architectural than symbolic value. Most American porticoes of the early years of the classical revival are supported by widely spaced pole-like columns which would have bewildered an ancient Greek had he been capable of recognizing them as recreations of Greek form.

Asher Benjamin, whose books furnished the designs for many of the builder-architects, thought that in all but the most pretentious of public buildings it was best to lighten the heavy parts of the orders "and thereby lighten the expense both of labour and materials." [35] He believed that the use of authentic Greek proportions of the Doric was utterly impractical in domestic structures.[36] He reported that the carpenters he questioned about their failure to follow strictly the classical orders answered that the Tuscan order was too heavy, the Ionic overrich, and the Doric very expensive, and that he felt obliged to design a column and entablature suitable to the tastes and purses of their employers.[37]

Sometimes the freedoms which American architects took with the historical forms led to original designs of austere strength, but more often the designers were satisfied with any sort of slap-dash approximation of those forms. All too frequently they were less interested in the formal than in the associational aspects of their buildings. To many romantic architects it seemed unrewarding and unnecessary to put very much effort into perfecting the proportions of their buildings when it was commonly believed that formal relations had no intrinsic importance. There was no strong incentive for laboring over refinements of design when any carelessly and crudely designed replica of a historic style would serve to arouse pleasant historical associations fully as well as the most subtly contrived formal composition.

If, on the one hand, the associational esthetic led to a relative unconcern for subtleties of formal design, on the other, an insistence upon the use of historically "correct" ornamental details developed. There was a general realization that literal imitations of historic buildings were appropriate for only a few monumental modern structures. But as time went on the archeological tendency grew more powerful and, as a rule, architects and lay critics insisted on faithfully copied detail. The science of archeology and the revival movement were twin children of the romantic interest in history; and American architects, usually without personal acquaintance with classical or Gothic buildings, copied their architectural details from works like Stuart and Revett's *The Antiquities of Athens*, and the volumes of Britton, Rickman, and the elder Pugin which pictured Medieval architecture, or from the handbooks which popularized the material in these works. The dryness of detail, characteristic of much revivalist architecture, is the result of too literal adherence to these books. And the use of ornamental details, copied from books, in conjunction with elements of a plain and functional nature often resulted in an inconsistent and discordant whole. The need for archeological correctness was in its effect upon architectural detailing directly contrary to the earlier romantic willingness to be satisfied with any association-producing token of a historical style. But, in the end, it had a similarly adverse effect upon overall design.

Notes

1. *Democracy in America,* in the translation of Henry Reeve, revised by Francis Bowen and Phillips Bradley (New York: Alfred A. Knopf, 1945), II, 51–52.

2. Although the thirst for esthetic simplicity of the early decades of the century primarily affected classical architecture, it had considerable influence upon the early buildings of the Gothic revival which were characterized by strongly emphasized horizontal lines, large areas of flat wall surface, and perfect symmetry.

3. *A Philosophical Inquiry into the Origin of our Ideas of the Sublime and Beautiful* in the *Works of Edmund Burke* (Boston, 1866), I, 148–150.

4. Letter from Paris, January 28, 1786 to Dr. James Currie, *The Papers of Thomas Jefferson,* IX, 240.

5. *Excursions in Italy* (Paris, 1838), 248–249. Cooper disregards Burke's distinction between the sublime and the beautiful but he exemplifies wonderfully the sense of the sublime in classical architecture.

6. *The Spectator,* vol. VII, no. 415 (New York, 1810), 151–152.

7. "The Arts and Artists," *loc. cit.,* 21.

8. *Essays on the Nature and Principles of Taste* (2nd ed.; Edinburgh, 1811), I, 359.

9. *Ibid.,* II, 139, 155–156, 157.

10. *Ibid.,* 195.

11. Payne Knight supported Alison's analysis except for arguing that light and color uniquely have an objective appeal apart from any associated ideas.

12. Cf. Benjamin, *Elements of Architecture* (Boston, 1843), 187, 203–204, and Lafever, *The Architectural Instructor* (New York, 1856), 16–17.

13. *The Diary of Philip Hone* (New York, 1927), I, 174.

14. *Art Hints* (London, 1855). 248.

15. *Notes in England and Italy* (New York, 1869), 407, 408. Mrs. Hawthorne's travel notes, though not published until 1869, were written between 1857 and 1859.

16. "Romantic Classicism in Architecture," *Gazette des Beaux Arts,* 6th series, XXV (Feb., 1944), 95–112.

17. For Gothic see Sir Kenneth Clark, *The Gothic Revival* (London: Constable, 1928), ch. III, "Ruins and Rococo." In the classic style, according to Kimball, the first use of complete temples was in the 1720's but as early as 1728 Batty Langley, who was hardly an innovator, suggested the use of sham ruihs in his *New Principles of Gardening.*

18. From the *Pocket Account Book* printed by Henry S. Randall in *The Life of Thomas Jefferson* (New York, 1858), I, 60, 61. The passage on the silent place in the trees is from some unidentified source.

19. Letter of April 16, 1805, which was cited by Fiske Kimball, "Latrobe's Designs for the Cathedral of Baltimore," *The Architectural Record,* vol. XLII, no. 6 (1917), 542.

20. Roger H. Newton, *Town and Davis* (New York: Columbia University Press, 1942), 81.

21. Cf. "The Protestant Plain Style Before 1630," *Journal of the Society of Architectural Historians,* vol. IX, no. 3 (1950), 5–6, 12.

22. See Karl Lehmann, *Thomas Jefferson: American Humanist* (New York: Macmillan, 1947), 52.

23. Letters to Latrobe, Oct. 10, 1809, and July 12, 1812, *Thomas Jefferson and the National Capitol,* edited by Saul K. Padover (Washington: United States Government Printing Office, 1946), 462, 471.

24. *Notions of the Americans,* II (Philadelphia, 1832), 193.

25. Letter to Madame La Comtesse de Tessé, *The Papers of Thomas Jefferson,* XI, 227–228. Cf. Wilbur Fisk, *Travels in Europe* (New York, 1838), 207.

26. (New York, 1856), 132.

27. *Cottage Residences* (2nd ed.; New York and London, 1844), 20.

28. For a discussion of the opposition between amateurs and professionals on the desirability of literal imitation of classical models see Talbot Hamlin, "The Greek Revival and Some of Its Critics," *The Art Bulletin,* vol. XXIV, no. 3 (1942), 244–258.

29. "Anniversary Oration," *Portfolio,* 3rd Series, vol. V, Appendix, 28.

30. *Greek Revival Architecture in America* (London, New York, Toronto: Oxford University Press, 1944), 70–71.

31. See excerpts from Biddle's diary reprinted in "Mr. Nicholas Biddle and the Architecture of Girard College," *Pennsylvania Magazine of History and Biography,* vol. XVIII, no. 3, 357.

32. Letter of April 22, 1807 printed in Padover, *Thomas Jefferson and the National Capitol,* 286–287.

33. *The Journal of Latrobe,* 139, 140. Latrobe wrote in a memoir appended to his design for the Second Bank of the United States "that nothing but the general character & style of the best Grecian Archiecure, can ever be preserved in such a design" because "the necessary arrangement of a house of business, requiring a multitude of apartments and abundant light, is so contrary to that of a Temple containing only an anteroom (Pronoas) a dark cell, and perhaps a few minor rooms for attendants"—reprinted by Fiske Kimball in "The Bank of the United States, 1818–1824," *Architectural Record,* vol. 58, no. 6 (1925), 584. William Strickland and Robert Mills, pupils of Latrobe, and Thomas U. Walter, a pupil of Strickland, all stressed the need of adapting classical features to modern functions; Strickland, "The Bank of the United States." *Analectic Magazine,* XIII (1819), 203; Mills, "The Progress of Architecture in Virginia," published in H. M. Pierce Gallagher, *Robert Mills* (New York: Columbia University Press, 1935), 155; Walter, "Architecture," *Journal of the Franklin Institute,* 3rd Series, vol. I, no. 1 (1841), 11–12.

34. The Second Bank of the United States (now part of the Independence National Historical Park), Philadelphia.

35. *The American Builder's Companion* (Boston, 1806), vi.

36. He wrote "a house having such an embellishment would not be less than twenty six feet in height. If it is to be of the Doric order, the example of the temple of Corinth would make the column four feet four inches in diameter and the entablature eight feet eight inches in height. No one could tolerate this proportion, since it would require the thickness of the column, at its base, to exceed the breadth of the doors and windows, and the entablature would cover one third of the front of the house"—*The Practical House Carpenter* (Boston, 1832), 102.

37. *The Practice of Architecture* (Boston, 1833), 34–35.

2
Romantic Naturalism: The Picturesque

ALTHOUGH THE FIRST ROMANTIC BUILDINGS—THE CLASSICAL COUNTRY HOUSES
and counting houses, Gothic churches and retreats—were descended from
garden structures, they reflected a lively historical imagination more than
sensitivity to the beauty of nature. Later romantic structures were increasingly shaped by a picturesque sense of form. This mode of perception, which
did reflect an affinity to natural forms, also originated in garden architecture.
It was the outgrowth of the great vogue of landscape painting which came
with the developing romantic sensibility. Buildings shaped by the picturesque
vision, nearly all of those built in the United States between 1845 and 1890,
have been the least understood in American architecture and until recently
have been almost universally scorned. Now it is becoming fashionable to
admire Victorian architecture and furniture. But twentieth century interest
in this art is curiously patronizing. Victorian buildings are regarded with a
mixture of wonder and condescension but rarely with the serious respect
accorded works of earlier periods. Contemporary taste may be charmed by
gems like the picturesque "little nookery somewhat in the Dutch style"
that Washington Irving used for a country retreat, but does not really
consider them works of art.

Explanation of the principles lying behind Irving's "Sunnyside," and

Sunnyside, Tarrytown, N.Y. (Photograph, Wayne Andrews)

kindred structures larger in scale and intention, may be found in English eighteenth century conceptions of garden design and rural architecture. Without some sense of the century-long English development of the picturesque esthetic, it is impossible to understand the sudden upheaval in American architecture in the 1830's and 1840's.

Inspired by seventeenth-century landscape painters, English garden designers and, later, architects became impatient with the formal symmetry of classical art. The first concentrated attack upon the symmetrical, axial garden of the seventeenth century with clipped trees, formal beds and "curious knots" was made in England by amateurs, literary men and connoisseurs of painting, rather than by professional gardeners. Between 1709 and 1713 the Earl of Shaftesbury, Addison, and Pope all expressed preference "for things of a natural kind." [1] Pope's own garden at Twickenham, which was constructed after 1719, embodied his theory hesitatingly and was the first garden of the eighteenth century to deliberately avoid formality.

Most prominent among the influences shaping the picturesque vision were the landscapes of painters of Italian scenes such as Claude Lorrain, Nicholas Poussin, Gaspar Dughet, and Salvator Rosa. The painterly attitude towards natural scenery was embodied by the chief writers on gardening in the late eighteenth century. They attacked as too artificial the wide lawns, smoothly rounded clumps, and broadly winding streams favored by Capability Brown, the leading garden designer of mid-century, and demanded that gardens be made picturesque; that is, like the carefully informal painted scenery of the landscape painters. Sir Uvedale Price developed the term picturesque into a separate category, midway between the awesome sublime and the placid beautiful of Burke, which consisted of "roughness and . . . sudden variation . . . joined to irregularity." [2]

By the end of the eighteenth century the lovers of the picturesque called for an irregular country house architecture which would harmonize with their picture-inspired naturalistic gardens.[3] Earlier in the century country houses placed in artfully informal grounds were designed with full Palladian formality. For the Burlington circle to follow nature in architecture had meant to build the architectural equivalent of the ordered, symmetrical system of Newton, while to follow nature in gardening meant to approximate the informality of natural scenery. But the three most influential writers on gardening and rural architecture at the end of the century, Price, Richard Payne Knight, and Humphry Repton, all advocated a degree of irregularity in rural architecture either in order that the house might be

arranged to take the maximum advantage of the best views of the garden
or so that it could be fused with the irregular landscaping of the garden.[4]
Knight, who was the strongest advocate of picturesque irregularity of the
three, had patterned his asymmetrical Downton Castle, which was built
about 1775, on the buildings which appeared in the landscapes of Claude
Lorrain.[5] Some years later G. L. Meason was to publish his *Landscape Architecture of the Great Painters of Italy*,[6] which comprised specimens of buildings from the works of painters of the Italian scene which the author thought
might serve as models for designers of irregular villas.

In the United States both garden design and rural architecture lagged
behind English example. Love of natural landscape was uncommon in
Colonial America. Perhaps the reality of the American struggle against the
wilderness discouraged attempts to sentimentalize nature. And, as late as
1796, upon his arrival in the United States, Latrobe was surprised to find
a formal flower garden beside the recently remodelled home of President
Washington. Although the garden seemed to him "the expiring groan . . .
of our grandfathers' pedantry,"[7] formal gardens continued to be laid out
in the United States well into the nineteenth century.

Among the earlier American projects for landscape gardens were Richard
Stockton's plan of copying Pope's garden at Twickenham for his country
place, Morven, near Princeton, New Jersey, and Jefferson's original scheme
for Monticello calling for a Palladian house placed in a landscape garden
which was to have romantic features such as benches of turf or rock, a grotto
spangled with translucent pebbles, and a "Gothic temple of antique
appearance."

Not until the thirties did the United States produce in Andrew Jackson
Downing a significant exponent of the English mode of garden design.
Downing, the son of a Hudson Valley nurseryman, had left school at sixteen
and educated himself with the aid of wealthy neighbors. Apparently he
became acquainted with the principles of picturesque landscape design
through extensive reading and conversations with English visitors. At the
time of his early death in 1852 in the burning of the Hudson steamer, *Henry
Clay*, he was the most influential of all American writers on country houses
and grounds. Downing's *Treatise on the Theory and Practice of Landscape
Gardening* (1841) was immediately and greatly popular, going through twelve
printings by 1860. The book found at the time of its publication, five years
after Emerson's *Nature* and about twenty years after the initial success of
Bryant and Cooper, a ready audience because of the almost universal Amer-

ican reverence for natural scenery. Downing's plan for romanticizing the official grounds in Washington was carried out by his successors, and rural suburbs were based upon his theories. New York's Central Park, designed by his protégé Calvert Vaux and Frederick Law Olmsted, was closely related to his picturesque mode of landscape design.

The first American architectural writer to advocate adapting the buildings erected in the country to their natural settings was John Haviland, who came to the United States from England in 1816 and made his name as a designer of prisons. His argument of 1821 differed in no important respect from the architectural theory of Price, Knight, and Repton at the turn of the century in England [8] and anticipated much of the later American literature on rural architecture. Haviland wrote that in the design of country houses "the style of the building should, in some measure . . . be adapted to or regulated by, the nature of the place, and the general growth of trees in it; the forms of the particular trees, which may be peculiar to it, the general character of the surrounding scenery; and the colour of the rocks as well as the ground." For "rocky exposed spots, where trees grow low and irregular," he suggested "low irregular edifices in the castle style"; and for other types of landscape he advised certain styles of architecture which would harmonize with them.[9] The architectural influence of the English proponents of the picturesque was shown a decade later in an article in the *New England Magazine*,[10] and in 1837 a small printing of a few numbers of a projected series of publications of picturesque designs, entitled *Rural Residences*, was published by Alexander Jackson Davis.

Of greater significance than these early manifestations of the spread of picturesque architectural theory in America was the chapter of Downing's *Treatise on the Theory and Practice of Landscape Gardening* devoted to buildings. A year later, in 1842, Downing published a book of plans for modest rural dwellings, *Cottage Residences*, with acknowledgments for designs and for assistance to Davis and John Notman, the pioneer American architects of asymmetrical houses. With this book began a flood of writing on picturesque rural architecture. During the next few decades books featuring plans and elevations of whole structures designed in the picturesque manner replaced as the most popular architectural publications the old carpenters' manuals,[11] which had been concerned primarily in showing untrained builders how to recreate in wood the ornamental details of monumental classical architecture of stone. The new volumes of house plans transformed the nature of architectural manuals and at the same time created

**Example of the Beautiful in Landscape Gardening from
Andrew Jackson Downing's** Landscape Gardening.

**Example of the Picturesque in Landscape Gardening from
Andrew Jackson Downing's** Landscape Gardening.

[Fig. 47. The Castellated Mode.]

The Castellated Mode from Andrew Jackson Downing's Landscape Gardening.

The Castellated Style. House of the Rev. Robert Bolton near New Rochelle, N.Y., from Andrew Jackson Downing's Landscape Gardening.

a revolution in the styles of rural buildings. Downing's most important architectural publication, *The Architecture of Country Houses*, appeared in 1850. Other significant volumes were Gervase Wheeler's *Rural Homes* (1851) and *Homes for the People* (1855), Lewis F. Allen's *Rural Architecture* (1852), and Calvert Vaux's *Villas and Cottages* (1857).[12]

"Does it make a good picture?" was the basic question asked of a building by the partisans of the picturesque. The architectural principles of these writers followed logically from their asking how a rural structure could be made to fuse with its natural surroundings as well as the painted architecture of Claude, Poussin, and Dughet did.[13] Although there was a widely held opinion that in peaceful, somewhat cultivated scenery, the designer was less restricted by the nature of the site than in wilder sections of the countryside,[14] a canon evolved as to what styles could compose well with the different types of natural scenery.[15] Downing divided all landscapes into the graceful and the picturesque types and divided architecture into two basic types to harmonize with his two varieties of landscape: the Greek, including the ancient Greek, the Roman, and the Italian; and the Gothic, which included the Tudor, the Flemish, the old English, and the castellated. Downing considered the bracketed cottage, the Swiss, and the Italian villa styles as intermediate between his two main categories of architecture. These types, he believed, were originally variations of the classical style and were suitable to graceful landscape when kept relatively simple and regular, but when made irregular were most useful in picturesque settings. There was general agreement among these writers that classical and Italian Renaissance styles of architecture, with their dominant horizontal lines and symmetrical arrangement combined with considerable refinement of detail, were most acceptable on level, peaceful sites covered with broad lawns and rich, fully rounded trees and shrubbery or near placid lakes.[16] For more varied, sloping terrain the Italian villa and Gothic styles were preferred, the Gothic especially where the foliage was thick and jagged, and the Italian style with its campanile where open spaces alternated with wooded places.[17] The favored styles for rocky mountainsides were the castellated and the Swiss chalet.[18]

Of these varied styles the most popular were the Italian villa, which was patterned after the irregular domestic architecture pictured by Claude and the Poussins in their paintings,[19] and the Tudor or Jacobean Gothic. The styles which went best with the extremes in scenery were less frequently used. Nostalgia for the heroic Medieval past was generally kept in check by middle class propriety. Few houses were built upon rocky crags, and there was some doubt about the suitability of the castellated style for peace-ful modern residences whose quiet inhabitants have "not the remotest idea of manifesting anything offensive or defensive to any of . . . [the] peace-loving neighborhood." [20] On the other hand, not many unimproved portions of the American countryside in the mid-nineteenth century seemed to pro-vide a proper setting for the classical styles of architecture, nor did the grounds improved by the romantic gardeners, and there was considerable prejudice against these styles entirely apart from considerations of site. Downing thought classical architecture suitable only for those with com-mon sense views; those with sentiment and feeling would, he believed, prefer the "poetic, aspiring, imaginative idea" of the Gothic.[21]

The notable irregularity of the Italian villa and rural Gothic styles goes far in explaining their popularity. To men who thought that "the great charm in the forms of natural landscape lies in . . . well-balanced irregu-larity," it seemed that such irregularity "is also the secret of success in every picturesque village . . . garden, country house or cottage." [22] As M. Field put it, "nature herself turns symmetry into picturesqueness; and in making a design picturesque, in the first instance, instead of regular, art is, after all, only imitating and increasing the effect of nature." [23]

Irregularity of both plan and silhouette was possible in the English and Italian rural styles. Irregularity in both was admired in itself and because it was productive of jagged patterns of light and shade which softened the three dimensional mass of a structure. Irregularity of plan was perfectly congruous in the rural Gothic and Italian villa styles because these styles were based on vernacular buildings of the past which frequently had an unsymmetrical character that would not have been tolerated in more formal architecture. An irregularity of plan was desirable, not only because it seemed to follow the scheme of nature and hence enable an irregular building to fuse more easily with its natural surroundings than would one more formally composed, but also because it would produce by its alternating projections and recesses "a variety of light and shadows, at different times of day, and from different points of view." [24] From the pictured architecture of the great landscapists of the seventeenth century, the theorists of the picturesque learned of the use of light and shade in rural architecture.[25] A varied inter-play of light and shadow could serve as well in actual landscapes as in painted ones to unite a building with the natural scenery around it. Later, shadows came to be valued in their own right, independently of any func-tion in relating architecture to setting. In the fifties one architect wrote that "the strength and character of a building depend almost wholly on the shadows which are thrown upon its surface by projecting members." [26]

Variety was one of the qualities which Price considered characteristic of the picturesque and which Downing thought of the greatest value in rural architecture.[27] The extremely varied and irregular skylines of the Italian villa and Tudor Gothic styles [28] were an important cause of the appeal of these styles for the picturesque architects. Downing was particularly fond of the Tudor roof line "abounding in the finer specimens with a rich variety of gables, turrets, buttresses, towers, and ornamental chimney-shafts, which form striking and spirited objects in domestic architecture, and harmonize agreeably with the hills and tree tops, and all the intricacy of outline in natural objects.[29] The Italian villas lacked many of the picturesque features of the rural Gothic skyline. They were without the gables which terminated the various extensions of the elaborate Gothic country house and without the turrets, parapets, or gabled dormers which served to break up broad areas of roof surface. But a considerable amount of diversity could be created on the roof line of an Italian villa by using a campanile and pavilions with roofs at different levels from the main one. The prime sources of the picturesque on the skylines of buildings in both these styles were the chimneys. Classicist architects of both the Palladian and classical revival movements had been embarrassed by northern chimneys, but the advocates of picturesque architecture gloried in them. "The handsome and curious stacks of chimneys" in Downing's phrase, "break and diversify the sky-outline of the building, enrich and give variety to its most bare and unornamented part." [30] Their vertical and irregular accents produced delightful patterns of light and shade and caused the top of the house to blend agreeably with the neighboring foliage.

The broadly projecting eaves of the Italian and the related Swiss and bracketed cottage styles were particularly admired by the rural architects. Eaves of three to four feet were preferred because they cast broad shadows across the elevations of a building, helping to remove any appearance of baldness it might have. Considerable attention was given to the members which supported the projecting eaves; they were a further source of variety in the region about the roof and were thought to suggest the idea of vigorous support.[31] Oliver P. Smith recommended brackets for large two-story houses with broad gables, consoles for high houses with hipped roofs, the fringe or ornamental barge and pendant for houses with steep gables, but concluded that "a change in the features and detail of these decorations, as they appear

The Tudor Gothic style. House of Joel Rathbone near Albany, N.Y., from Andrew Jackson Downing's Landscape Gardening.

Italian villa style. House of Bishop Doane, Burlington, N. J., by John Notman, from Andrew Jackson Downing's Landscape Gardening.

in different positions on the same structure, is not only unobjectionable, but really desirable, since variety is always essential to picturesque beauty." [32]

The sides as well as the roofs of country houses were made picturesque. Everything possible was done to avoid the monotony of plain broad surfaces. On the walls, themselves, the clapboards, which had been traditionally used in the United States since the seventeenth century, came under attack. Some argued that they produced a kind of shading of their own which interfered with the principal shadows and neutralized the picturesque effect of overhanging eaves, mouldings, and other projecting features.[33] Downing recommended that clapboards be replaced by wide, unplaned, vertical boards covered with thin strips at the place they joined. This method of building seemed to him to have "a character of strength and permanence" lacking in the old system.[34] Certainly the use of unplaned boards and the narrow, vertical strips gave the wall a varied surface texture attracting the eye to it as did the use in stone walls of material which had "variety of color and irregularity of strata." [35] Thus the spectator was induced to concentrate on the surface rather than the geometric mass of the building. Other devices were used to give prominence to the surface of the walls; in the Gothic cottages the great variety in the shapes and sizes of the windows, which were often filled with mullions or lattice work tracery, drew the spectators' attention. Hoods and mouldings of considerable prominence were used around the windows and doors of Italian type houses preventing these openings from appearing as mere holes in the walls of a block.[36] The shadows cast by the hoods and other members also helped to concern the eye with the surface of the structure.

The picturesque treatment of the walls did not stop with the handling of the openings and of the surface itself. Various elements were used which projected from the walls, breaking up the plain broad surfaces and incidentally adding additional shadows to those cast by the eaves and the lesser mouldings. Porches, more popular in this country than in England, were common in both the Tudor Gothic and Italian villa styles, although in the latter style they often took the form of recessed arcades. Bay or oriel windows were also used to enliven the façades, and balconies and terraces with balustrades were specialties of the Italian style. All these features broke down the geometrical quality of country houses and helped to make them harmonize with the irregular natural forms around them.

The picturesque point of view affected the color as well as the form of rural architecture. Fenimore Cooper, in *Home as Found* (1838), criticized the universal American custom of painting houses white.[37] But Downing was the first American architectural writer to echo the picturesque color theories of Reynolds, Price, and Wordsworth.[38] Downing first published his theory of color in his earliest purely architectural book, *Cottage Residences* (1842), and by the end of the decade his ideas dominated fashionable practice,[39] having been taken up with slight modifications by all the other writers on rural architecture.

White paint which, through the neo-classic desire to imitate stone buildings in wood, had become almost universal for wooden structures in America was roundly attacked. Downing's protégé, Calvert Vaux, declared that a white house with green blinds is "clearly projected from the surrounding landscape . . . instead of harmonizing with it." "This lack of sympathy between the building and its surroundings," seemed to him, "very disagreeable to an artistic eye." [40] The custom of painting brick or wooden buildings a bright red color was criticized by Lewis F. Allen on similar grounds.[41]

Downing pointed out the example of the landscape painters to prospective builders of rural homes. He remarked that no landscape painter of any prominence "was ever guilty of displaying in his pictures a glaring white house, but, on the contrary the buildings introduced by the great masters have uniformly a mellow softened shade of color, in exquisite keeping with the surrounding objects." [42]

From the practice of the landscape painters Downing turned to the practice of nature herself for hints for the rural architect. Nature no more than Claude or Poussin used glaring colors. "In natural landscape, anything like strong and bright colors is seldom seen, except in very minute portions, and least of all pure white—chiefly appearing in small objects like flowers." To Downing it seemed that "the practical rule which should be deduced from this, is, to avoid all those colors which nature avoids. In building we should copy those that she offers chiefly to the eye—such as those of soil, rocks, wood, and the bark of trees—the materials of which houses are built. These materials offer us the best and most natural study from which harmonious colors for the houses themselves should be taken." [43]

The picturesque esthetic demanded that a house harmonize with its natural surroundings, but it also demanded that the blocky forms of the house be minimized by the play of light and shade. The desire for shadows tempered considerably the wish that a building should resemble in color its natural surroundings. The green of foliage and other dark colors were impossible because they killed the effect of shadows cast upon the walls.

Downing pointed out that houses are not constructed of leaves or grass.[44] Most of the other writers followed his lead in advocating the use of light colors patterned on natural building materials. Favorites included the colors of granite, free-stone, brownstone, and slate, as well as colors suggested by russet stones, oak, soft wood, and straw. Other colors frequently praised were fawn and drab.[45] Related to the preference for these colors on wooden houses was Downing's recommendation of the light brown sand-stone or free-stone of Connecticut and New Jersey and the light gray Cincinnati stone because they combine well with foliage.[46]

Picturesque theory required that porches, window mouldings, blinds, brackets, and other such elements be emphasized to eliminate the unnatural monotony of plain broad surfaces. Downing thought that such features "confer the same kind of expression on a house that the eyes, eyebrows, lips, etc., do upon the human countenance." He advised painting the details a different color from the rest of the house because "to paint the whole house plain drab, gives it very much the same dull and insipid effect that colorless features (white hair, pale eye-brows, lips, etc., etc.) do the face." [47] Since the main walls were painted in light colors against which shadows would be effective, the details had to be done in darker ones. Either a different color or a darker shade of the same color was acceptable for the decorative features.[48] Both alternatives were satisfactory from the picturesque point of view; both drew additional attention to those features which tended to destroy the cubic aspect of the building.

The architectural revolution engendered by Downing and the other advocates of the picturesque brought a radical change to the shapes and plans of ordinary American houses, the first really profound change since the introduction of classical principles in the last quarter of the seventeenth century. For nearly a hundred and seventy-five years regularity, simplicity, and symmetry had been the ideals of American builders. Now the picturesque taste made geometrical regularity of form an anathema. Houses burst out of the traditional rectangular moulds in varied shapes and in many directions. Irregularity grew in the interior arrangement of spaces as well as in the creation of arrestingly jagged exterior silhouettes. The classical insistence upon symmetry of ordered elements steadily lost force. Downing expressed the new feeling for asymmetrical design, writing that in satisfactory irregular compositions "there is a kind of hidden proportion which one half of the whole bears to the other." [49] As early as 1835 Alexander Jackson Davis ex-

Project for a Gothic Villa. Drawing by Alexander Jackson Davis, courtesy of the New York Historical Society.

Project for an Italian Villa. Drawing by Alexander Jackson Davis,
location unknown; rephotographed courtesy of Columbia University Press.

hibited an architectural drawing in which he had endeavored to balance a tall chimney, an oriel window, and a carriage porch on the right side of a Gothic house against a steep turret and an entrance porch at the left. A more successful example of asymmetrical design is the Italian villa which Davis made in 1851 for Llewellyn Haskell, wholesale druggist and patron of Llewellyn Park. Here a campanile to the left of the nearly central pavilion subtly plays against the broader expanse of roof and wall and the extra windows on the right.

An architectural development of the nineteenth century, perhaps even more important than the break from the classical tradition of symmetrical composition, was the spread of functionalist theories of structure and ornament. Vincent Scully, the foremost student of picturesque wooden architecture, puts particular emphasis upon the elements of functionalism in the theories of Downing and his fellows. He stresses the "romantic rationalism" of Downing's discussion of wooden construction,[50] citing a passage where Downing recommends vertical instead of horizontal siding for wooden frame houses "because it has an expression of strength and truthfulness which the other has not. The main timbers which enter into the frame of a wooden house and support the structure are vertical, and hence the vertical boarding signifies to the eye a wooden house." [51]

Scully is certainly justified in emphasizing the functional as well as picturesque aspects of Downing's theory. A generation earlier Latrobe had combined functional and esthetic arguments for the use of simple geometric neo-classical forms. Now Downing, Gervase Wheeler [52] and the others united arguments based on both functional and esthetic considerations in support of irregular, asymmetrical picturesque forms. In all his books Downing stressed the importance of expression of purpose in domestic architecture. To him, "verandas, piazzas, porches, balconies, clustered chimneys, [and] window-blinds" all seemed demanded by "significance, fitness and propriety," [53] in order to inform the observer that a building was used for domestic purposes. Significantly these features not only served to indicate the building's function but also contributed to its picturesque character. The need to shed snow during the cold northern winter was used as an argument for the adoption of the jagged Gothic roofs favored by the picturesque taste.[54] The broad projecting eaves of the Italian villa style were recommended against the hot summer sun of the American South,[55] and also against Northern storms, "ever changing from snow to rain." [56] The ground plans as well as the other architectural features favored by the picturesque architects were defended on the grounds of practicality. The functional advantages of an irregular layout were repeatedly stressed.[57]

At first the principles of picturesque architectural design were applied exclusively to country houses. But eventually these principles were so widely accepted that buildings very different in style and setting were regarded from the picturesque point of view. Chester Hills, Minard Lafever, and William H. Ranlett all applied conceptions derived from picturesque theory to classical architecture. As early as 1834 Hills attributed the superiority of the Greek style over the Roman to the careful design of the various parts of the Greek order on the basis of the ellipsis, parabola, or hyperbola so that masses of middle tint, "broad qualities of light, relieved by striking depths of shadows and sparkling effects" would prevail, whereas the Roman Doric was composed in a complicated way of small circular parts which produced a monotonously even mixture of light, middle tint, and shadow.[58] Lafever was particularly attracted by the shade producing qualities of the Doric capital and fluted columns.[59] Ranlett deplored the lack of shade catching sculpture on the tympanums of Greek Revival pediments.[60]

In addition to influencing nineteenth-century ideas of classical architecture, picturesque principles moved from the countryside into city streets over-turning traditional American conceptions of town planning. At first, the American writers had followed Payne Knight in drawing a distinction between what was architecturally appropriate for the city and for the country. In 1841 Downing thought that for "a city or town or its immediate vicinity, where space is limited, where buildings stand crowded together, and depend for their attractions entirely upon the style and manner of their construction, mere [formal] architectural effect, after convenience and utility are consulted, is of course the only point to keep in view." [61]

Later, picturesque theories of design were carried into the suburbs and into the city itself. Gervase Wheeler suggested using a campanile in conjunction with a rectangular villa for suburban sites which necessitated a regular form for the structure, the height and proportion of the tower to be such as would give a pyramidal shape to the mass. The building would then rise in a series of set-backs from the foundation; the first at the small break of the base near the ground, another in the lines of the veranda roofs, the next at the main roof of the structure, and the final in the culmination of the overhanging canopy of the tower. Thus, he wrote, "the summit outline becomes . . . broken, and the same play of light and shade is secured

Castlewood House, Llewellyn Park. Engraving from New York Illustrated News, 1860.

The Atheneum, Philadelphia. (Photograph, Wayne Andrews)

as if the ground permitted of marked breaks and projections of the plan." [62]

With the triumph of the picturesque came a concerted attack upon traditional urban architecture and town planning. The old fashioned city streets lined with geometrically regular façades placed in parallel lines seemed dull to those who wished to enliven urban buildings with irregularity and shadow-producing projections. The earlier American city, organized about a rectangular green with streets laid out in a gridiron pattern and filled with trim, box-like houses, had been a provincial echo of the great ordered Baroque city plans of Europe. These plans had been imitated in Charleston, Annapolis, Williamsburg, and Philadelphia, the chief American communities founded in the late seventeenth century. The Baroque idea of order seemed to the new taste of the mid-nineteenth century mechanical and most unpicturesque. The new ideal in town-scaping was reflected in rural suburbs like Davis's Llewellyn Park, created out of a tract of undulating New Jersey hillside with stone gate lodges, rustic bridges over the streams, and a wide enough variety of houses to make up an anthology of rural architecture.[63]

Despite the growing impatience with the inherited methods of designing street architecture, full picturesque irregularity was slow in appearing in civic and commercial buildings. Between 1851 and 1865 Thomas U. Walter was extending the national Capitol in accordance with its original neo-classical style. The picturesque asymmetry of James Renwick's Smithsonian Institution was unusual among public buildings of the pre-Civil War era. The most popular new mode for civic architecture was the Renaissance palazzo style, initiated in England by Sir Charles Barry. Notable among American examples of the style were John Notman's Atheneum in Philadelphia (1847) and two buildings in Boston, the Atheneum (1847) and the Old Public Library (1858). These structures patterned after the urban architecture of the Renaissance seem far removed from the irregular rural buildings then going up all over the American countryside, yet in important ways they reflect picturesque principles of design. The palazzo type façade with heavy cornice, prominent string courses, rusticated and groined masonry, and hooded or pedimented windows was far richer and more plastic than the flat, precise façades favored in the American classical revivals. Increasingly bold and coarse elements were adopted, and the play of light and shade was an important factor considered in the design of these buildings. The architect of the Atheneum in Boston was criticized for failing to make his projecting members sufficiently bold. It was thought that the building needed "a little more of what John Ruskin calls 'the Rembrandtism of architecture.' " [64] Eventually, as a taste for rougher and more intricate effects developed, Venetian designs, notably Sansovino's library, replaced the severer Roman palazzos as the most favored models.[65]

Contemporaneous with the growing popularity of the palazzo style was the displacement of granite by brown sandstone as the standard material for masonry structures. Picturesque principles affected the materials as well as the models used in urban architecture. Granite, a material favored by classical revivalists, lost favor because it did not take shadows well. Brownstone's dramatic response to patterns of light and shade made it seem ideal. One contemporary critic praised its warm color "which takes the sunshine with a quiet elegance." "Moreover [he remarked] . . . admirably suited as it is for large and massive buildings such as stores and churches, [it] is of so fine a quality and so delicate a tone, that no fine work is thrown away upon it." [66]

During the third quarter of the nineteenth century picturesque principles dominated architectural practice in cities as well as in the country, in public buildings as in private dwellings. C. L. V. Meeks has suggested the picturesque as an inclusive category, comparable to Wölfflin's renaissance and baroque, to define the essential character of all nineteenth-century architecture. Mr. Meeks sets up five qualities of the picturesque: roughness, movement, irregularity, variety, and intricacy, and relates them to Wölfflin's five characteristics of the baroque. He takes Geoffrey Scott to task for approving of the baroque, which Scott saw as a blend of the picturesque and the classical, and condemning the picturesque. Scott, he writes, "in what may have been the first tentative manifestation of the picturesque . . . can tolerate it, but as it matures he loses sympathy with it." [67] Meek's argument brings up interesting questions about the nature of picturesque architecture, its relation to the baroque, and its ultimate esthetic value, which can be only briefly treated at the end of this chapter.

Perhaps the best way to summarize the effect which the picturesque movement had on architecture is to analyze the alterations made on an old building to bring it up to date. Calvert Vaux published an account, with many illustrations, of his firm's transformation of an old-fashioned, vaguely classical house, which had a blocky addition, into a properly picturesque building. The principal changes, apart from placing a gable roof on the addition so that it came up to the roof level of the main house, were to destroy the regularity and symmetry of the original structure,

SOUTH-EAST VIEW BEFORE ALTERATION.

NORTH-WEST VIEW AS ALTERED.

SOUTH-EAST VIEW AS ALTERED.

Alterations of a farm house by Downing and Vaux.
Engraving from Calvert Vaux's Villas and Cottages.

to break up the blocky appearance of the building with square projections to the rear and on the opposite side "in front of the depth of the veranda," and to enliven the walls and the roofs with hooded and bay windows, wide-eaved dormers, chimney stacks, and a cupola-type ventilator. In addition, "the roof was projected all around and fitted with brackets," and "the verandas were somewhat improved" by adding brackets and more complex supports.[68] Of particular interest is the bull's-eye dormer which carries the line of the wall up onto the roof, breaking up, even more effectively than did the overhanging eaves and brackets, the clear distinction between those two elements that had existed in the old house.

The picturesque alterations clearly added qualities to the building that can be equated with Meek's five, roughness, movement, irregularity, variety, and intricacy. However, it seems to me that these five categories fail to include an essential characteristic of picturesque architecture, which differentiates it from both classical and baroque architectures, its concern with surface rather than with the moulding of either form or space. A most significant difference between this house before the alteration and after is the loss of simple three-dimensional form and the gain of an intricate, varied, interest-catching surface. Over-concern with surface remained characteristic of picturesque architecture until its final phase. Oddly enough, the result of constantly increasing the plasticity of parts was a loss in the plastic feeling of the whole. Surface elements became more and more three-dimensional but usually they were so varied and restless that they failed to mould either exterior mass or interior space in coherent fashion.

The picturesque, like the baroque, abolished the sharp separation between forms that was characteristic of classical architecture, and it, too, depended upon contrasting patterns of light and shade to achieve its desired effects. But there are great differences between the results produced through somewhat similar methods. In the baroque the integrity of the individual forms was sacrificed in order to get a more unified plastic whole, and the play of light and shade was one of the devices used to bring this about. Generally speaking, the effect of light and shadow upon baroque façades, such as that of Pietro da Cortona's church of Santa Maria della Pace at Rome, is to emphasize the essential parts of the overall design and to obscure the points of junction between them. But in contrast, picturesque structures like Richard Upjohn's intricate "Kingscote," built in 1841 in Newport, have no overall unity similar to that of the baroque in which the various irregular elements are subordinated.[69] Light and shade are used to

Santa Maria della Pace, Rome. (Photograph, Anderson)

Kingscote, Newport, R.I. (Photograph, Robert Merservey)

neutralize rather than bring out the more prominent masses of form. Intricacy and variety are delighted in at the expense of general coherence, and the function of the patches of light and shadow which are cast across the façade is to cut up the main elements of the design, reducing its three-dimensional quality and preventing the possibility of monotonous plain surfaces.

This *horror vacui* deprived picturesque architecture of sufficient emphases to give it completely satisfactory unity or order. Typical was the advice given to wealthy builders of Elizabethan houses by Mrs. L. C. Tuthill who suggested that the more prominent portions of a design must not be finished in a way that "would have attracted the eye by itself without being placed in a conspicuous situation" lest "the united attraction of form and detail" draw the attention entirely to the emphasized parts. "Consequently the parts that project and are to bear a strong light, must be chiselled with infinite delicacy; but those parts which are to be flat and in shade, should be marked with great sharpness and boldness, that the impression may be equalized." [70] When the explicit aim of a school of architects was to cause all parts of their buildings to make equally strong impressions, it is easy to see why these buildings have baffled modern taste.

Notes

1. Shaftesbury's *The Moralists* (London, 1727), II, 393–394; Addison's *The Spectator*, nos. 412, 414, and 477 for June 9, June 25, and September 6, 1712; Pope's *The Guardian*, no. 173, September 29, 1713. For discussion of the development of the love of unadorned nature in the early eighteenth century see Elizabeth W. Manwaring, *Italian Landscape in Eighteenth Century England* (New York, 1925), 122–127; Christopher Hussey, *The Picturesque* (London and New York: G. P. Putnam's Sons, 1927), 128–129; Nikolaus Pevsner, "The Genesis of the Picturesque," *Architectural Review*, vol. XCVI, no. 575 (1944), 139–143.

2. *Sir Uvedale Price on the Picturesque* (Edinburgh and London, 1842), 82.

3. For discussions of the picturesque in architecture see Hussey, *op. cit.*, ch. VI; Nikolaus Pevsner, "Richard Payne Knight," *The Art Bulletin*, vol. XXXI, no. 4 (1949), especially Appendix I and pages 293–296.

4. Hussey, *op. cit.*, 209–215.

5. Pevsner, "Richard Payne Knight," *loc. cit.*, 296.

6. (London, 1828). Charles Parker's *Villa Rustica* (London, 1832, 1833, 1848) contained designs based on actual rural Italian buildings.

7. *The Journal of Latrobe*, 52.

8. In England interest in picturesque architecture slackened after the period of Price and Knight. No important publications appeared between 1807 and 1823—Hussey, *op. cit.*, 222–229. The picturesque movement in America was associated with the second wave of the picturesque in England, the leaders of which were John C. Loudon and Peter F. Robinson.

9. *The Practical Builders' Assistant* (2nd ed.; Baltimore, 1830), Bk. III, 36–37. Compare Price's "Essay on Architecture and Buildings," of 1798, in Sir Thomas D. Lauder's *Sir Uvedale Price on the Picturesque* (Edinburgh and London, 1842), 328, 334, and Humphry Repton, *Fragments on the Theory and Practice of Landscape Gardening*, in John C. Loudon's *The Landscape Gardening and Landscape Architecture of the late Humphry Repton* (London, 1840), 413.

10. Vol. II (January, 1832), 30–36.

11. Henry-Russell Hitchcock, *American Architectural Books* (3rd rev. ed.; Minneapolis: University of Minnesota Press, 1946), iii.

12. Hitchcock lists thirteen printings of *Cottage Residences*, seven before 1861; nine printings of *The Architecture of Country Houses*, six before 1861; nine printings of *Rural Homes*, six before 1861; six printings of *Homes for the People*, four before 1861; eight printings of *Rural Architecture*, five before 1861; and six printings of *Villas and Cottages*—*ibid.*, pp. 2, 31–32, 108–109, 113–114.

13. Price's "Essay on Architecture and Buildings" is the first full statement of this.

14. Gervase Wheeler wrote: "If the range of vision be limited, the scenery quiet, and possessing a self-contained charm of beauty or grandeur complete in itself, the character of the House may be left more to the bent of the owner's taste, than were the building a prominent feature in an extended range of landscape. . . . The house . . . may be more forcefully developed, more profuse in details and more whimsical. . . . [Where the building is linked to extended landscape] every feature must accord with the prevailing character of the natural forms around, and the details and architectural features must be bolder, more marked and expressive, in order to be defined by the eye that views them after a scale formed upon the bold fragments of nature's architecture"—*Rural Homes* (Auburn and Rochester, N.Y., 1853), 58.

15. Humphry Repton probably originated the idea of adapting the style of a country house to its landscape setting, and the idea was developed by his follower, John C. Loudon; see Repton's *Fragments on the Theory and Practice of Landscape Gardening* (1816) reprinted by Loudon in *The Landscape Gardening and Landscape Architecture of the Late Humphry Repton* (London, 1840), 413, and Loudon's *Encyclopedia of Cottage, Farm and Villa Architecture* (1833) (London, 1839 ed.), 773.

16. *A Treatise on Landscape Gardening* (New York, 1844), 349–351; Wheeler, *Rural Homes*, 57, 66–67; "The Architects and Architecture of New York," *Brother Jonathan*, vol. V, no. 6 (June 10, 1843), 151.

17. Lewis F. Allen, *Rural Architecture* (New York, 1852), 23; "The Architects and Architecture of New York," *loc. cit.*, 151; Downing, *Cottage Residences* (New York, 1844), 151–152.

18. *Ibid.;* Allen, *op. cit.*, 23; Downing, *Landscape Gardening*, 362, 368, 375. In this case the traditional associations of these styles with rugged mountain scenery seem to have been as influential as purely picturesque considerations. Cf. Downing as cited above.

19. Henry-Russell Hitchcock suggests "a vague but complex legend" to account for the forms of a notable Italian villa. "Part of the walls would have been the ruins of a Roman villa; these the Middle Ages repaired, adding a round and a square tower for defense, the Renaissance introduced long oblong windows for light and air, and also surrounded the main square block with an elegant arched loggia." *Early Victorian Architecture in Britain* (New Haven: Yale University Press, 1954), I, 27.

20. Downing, "Hints to Persons about Building in the Country," his introduction to George Wightwick's *Hints to Young Architects* (New York and London, 1847), xvi.

21. *The Architecture of Country Houses* (New York, 1851), 262–263.

22. Calvert Vaux, "Hints for Country House Builders," *Harper's New Monthly Magazine*, vol. XI, no. LXVI (1855), 763.

23. *Rural Architecture* (New York, 1857), 118. Calvert Vaux argued that the American atmosphere furnished additional reason for unsymmetrical design. It is lacking in humidity and "dry air is so transparent that it permits a distinctness of outline to objects, even at a considerable distance from the eye. . . . The light in America being therefore powerful and somewhat trying to the eye . . . it would seem that we ought to avoid square,

monotonous masses, and regular extent in American rural architecture; because the climate rarely supplies the shifting, mellow light in which such simple forms appear to advantage" —"Hints for Country House Builders," *loc. cit.,* 771–772. Vaux ignores the fact that classical architecture originated in an atmosphere at least as clear as the American, but in all probability his idea of classical architecture in its native setting was based on the painted Italian landscapes of the seventeenth and eighteenth centuries.

24. M. Field, *Rural Architecture* (New York, 1857), 102.

25. Price wrote that "the architect of buildings in the country should be *architto-pittore;* for, he ought . . . not only to be acquainted with the principles, but, as far as design goes, with the practice of landscape painting." Price delighted in the play of light and shade about clustered Gothic chimneys and wrote of Ostade's cottages that they are "not so much to be valued on their own account, as from being productive of what these painters most excelled in, variety of light and shadow"—*Sir Uvedale Price on the Picturesque,* 329, 352, 392.

26. Henry W. Cleaveland, William Backus and Samuel D. Backus, *Village and Farm Cottages* (New York, 1856), 96.

27. *The Architecture of Country Houses,* 16.

28. For the sake of simplicity and clarity I have ignored the multiple minor distinctions between the Tudor, Elizabethan and rural Gothic, etc. and the Swiss, bracketed cottage, and Italian villa styles, etc. and have included all of the first group under the term Tudor or rural Gothic and all of the second group under the term Italian villa or bracketed style.

29. *Cottage Residences,* 67–68.

30. *A Treatise on Landscape Gardening,* 346.

31. *The Architecture of Country Houses,* 113, 114. John Coolidge in his study of the early nineteenth-century architecture of Lowell, *Mill and Mansion,* traced the evolution of brackets or consoles through three stages from small, evenly spaced, horizontal ones through large, dripping ones that were usually paired to ones which secured an effect of unemphatic ornateness—(New York: Columbia University Press, 1942), 85–86.

32. *The Domestic Architect* (Buffalo, 1852), 33.

33. Cleaveland, Backus and Backus, *op. cit.,* 97.

34. *Rural Essays* (New York, 1853), 249–250.

35. Cf. J. Coleman Hart, *Designs for Parish Churches* (New York, 1857), 25.

36. Downing, *The Architecture of Country Houses,* 88, and *Rural Essays,* 249; Vaux, *Villas and Cottages* (New York, 1857), 71–73. The picturesque designers' fear that the openings might appear as mere holes in the wall illuminates the difference in their point of view from that of the classical revivalists, the extremists among whom resented having to use windows at all. A writer in the *New York Mirror* deplored the effect of all windows except skylights because "they break in upon that majesty and solemn repose that would otherwise rest on the broad and massive wall." Vol. V (March 1, 1828), 271.

37. Fenimore Cooper, *Home as Found* (Philadelphia, 1838), 147.

38. Reynolds is supposed to have said, "if you would fix upon the best color for your house, turn up a stone, or pluck a handful of grass by the roots, and see what is the color of the soil where the house is to stand, and let that be your choice"—cited by Downing, *The Architecture of Country Houses,* 201. Price's attack on the use of white paint in his *Essay on the Picturesque* (1794) was very influential. He objected to the use of bright red and glaring white coloring for rural buildings because glare destroys the effects of breadth in landscape; he pointed with approval to the mellow colors used by Claude and other landscape painters—ch. VII, *Sir Uvedale Price on the Picturesque,* 124–133. Wordsworth wrote in his "Guide through the District of the Lakes" (1810) that "the objections to white as a colour, in large spots or in masses of landscape, especially in mountainous country are insurmountable." He recommended as "the safest colour for general use . . . something between a cream and a dust-colour"—*The Prose Works of Willam Wordsworth* (London, 1896), II, 74–75. These latter two were also cited by Downing, Price in *Cottage Residences,* 23, and Wordsworth in *The Architecture of Country Houses,* 200.

39. In the late forties William H. Ranlett attacked the recent and fashionable custom "of painting houses . . . dull and sombre hues"—*The Architect* (New York, 1847–49), 50; see also Allen, *Rural Architecture,* 42–43.

40. "Hints for Country House Builders," *loc. cit.,* 773.

41. *Rural Architects,* 47.

42. *Cottage Residences,* 23.

43. *The Architecture of Country Houses,* 200.

44. *Ibid.,* 200–201. For houses placed in groves of trees Downing would tolerate even the detested white paint.

45. For color suggestions see: Downing, *The Architecture of Country Houses,* 200–204; "The Architects and Architecture of New York," *Brother Jonathan,* vol. V, no. 12 (July 22, 1843), 331–332; Ranlett, *The Architect,* 50; Allen, *Rural Architecture,* 42–43; Wheeler, *Rural Homes,* 157; Lafever, *The Architectural Instructor,* 442–444; Field, *Rural Architecture,* 31.

46. *The Architecture of Country Houses,* 67.

47. *Ibid.,* 204.

48. *Ibid.;* Vaux, "Hints for Country House Builders," *loc. cit.,* 775.

49. *Cottage Residences,* 28.

50. "Romantic Rationalism and the Expression of Structure in Wood. Downing, Wheeler, Gardner, and the 'Stick Style,' 1840–1876," *The Art Bulletin,* vol. XXXV, no. 2 (1953), especially 123–135.

51. *The Architecture of Country Houses,* 51–52.

52. Scully, *loc. cit.,* 135–137.

53. "Hints to Persons about Building in the Country," *loc. cit.,* xvi.

54. Downing, *Cottage Residences,* 107.

55. Downing, *The Architecture of Country Houses,* 265, 313.

56. Downing, "Hints to Persons about Building in the Country," *loc. cit.,* xxi.

57. Downing, *A Treatise on Landscape Gardening,* 359, 372 and *Cottage Residences,* 68, 155; Oliver P. Smith, *The Domestic Architect,* 30; Field, *Rural Architecture,* 17; "The Architects and Architecture of New York," *Brother Jonathan,* vol. V, no. 6 (June 10, 1843), 152.

58. *The Builder's Guide* (Hartford, 1834), 8.

59. *The Architectural Instructor,* 366.

60. *The Architect,* 77.

61. *A Treatise on Landscape Gardening,* 340; cf. Mrs. L. C. Tuthill, *A History of Architecture* (Philadelphia, 1848), 281–282; Field, *Rural Architecture,* 18–19; Wheeler, *Rural Homes,* 109.

62. *Homes for the People* (New York, 1855), 43–44.

63. Newton, *Town and Davis,* 107, 269, 280–286.

64. Thomas C. Clarke, "Architects and Architecture," *The Christian Examiner,* vol. XLIX, no. 161 (1850), 284.

65. This was particularly true of commercial architecture. Cast iron fronts were often designed in a loosely Venetian manner. Cf. Hitchcock, *Early Victorian Architecture in Britain,* 173.

66. "New York Daguerreotyped," *Putnam's Monthly,* vol. I, no. 2 (1853), 126.

67. "Picturesque Eclecticism," *The Art Bulletin,* vol. XXXII, no. 3 (1950), 226–235. See also his *The Railroad Station* (New Haven: Yale University Press, 1956), 1–11.

68. I infer from Vaux's account that this alteration was made when Downing was still alive and active in the firm, Downing and Vaux. Cf. *Villas and Cottages,* 205–210.

69. Meeks differs sharply. He writes of "the prime importance of the plasticity of the whole, an over-all concept congenial to modern thought and essential to the understanding of the composition of nineteenth century buildings which should be seen as made up of many interlocking parts, not as unrelated, planimetric façades"—"Picturesque Eclecticism," *loc. cit.,* 228.

70. *History of Architecture,* 304–305.

3
Nature, the Gothic, and Functionalism

DURING THE 1830'S THE PREDOMINANCE OF BUILDINGS ERECTED IN THE GREEK style in the United States was such that the Greek revival seemed to many to be the national style. Yet in this decade Gothic structures were designed in considerable numbers for churches, homes, colleges, and a variety of public purposes. And in the decades following, Gothic buildings came to outnumber classical ones.

Prominent among the causes of the American fascination with Medieval structures was the continuing interest in the Gothic novelists, "Monk" Lewis and Ann Radcliffe. But more important were the romances of Walter Scott, which created a deeply felt want for a romantic Medieval past. One result of the cult of Scott was the fostering by William Alexander Caruthers and John Pendleton Kennedy of the myth of a quasi-feudal aristocratic seventeenth-century Virginia and Maryland in novels such as *The Cavaliers of Virginia* (1834–35), and *Rob of the Bowl* (1838). But as early as 1832 Alexander Jackson Davis had created outside Baltimore "Glen Ellen," a Gothic "castle" complete with a tracery-filled oriel window, octagonal corner turrets, and a mock ruin for a gate house. Davis's client, Robert Gilmor, notable art collector and patron of American artists, had recently returned from a visit to the master of "Abbotsford."

Even more important, ultimately, to the popularity of the Gothic style than the Scott-inspired nostalgia for the Middle Ages was the growing tendency to associate Gothic buildings with nature. Nineteenth-century Americans came to think of their nation, the land of Natty Bumpo, as nature's nation in contrast to the corrupt and effete civilizations of Europe. America might lack a Medieval past but it certainly did not lack unspoiled natural scenery as romancers like Cooper and Simms and landscape painters from Cole to Bierstadt were intent on showing the world. Any style of architecture which could be acclaimed as the natural style was a style to be reckoned with in nineteenth-century America.

In the years before the full influence of romantic naturalism was felt, the cause of Gothic architecture had been advanced by both the fashionable taste for sublimity and the new picturesque esthetic. Edmund Burke had seen sublimity in Gothic buildings [1] and his view became general in America by the second quarter of the nineteenth century. Although all revivals of monumental historic styles were influenced by the picturesque principles of design, the Gothic gained most support from them. Because of their slow construction over extended periods of time, the major Gothic structures of Europe had an irregularity and a variety of style highly pleasing to the picturesque taste.

Oddly enough, despite American travellers' delight in the irregularity of great Medieval cathedrals like Chartres, Rouen, and Ely, few of the monumental buildings erected in the early decades of the Gothic revival showed asymmetrical characteristics or much picturesque variation. Notably regular Medieval structures were usually used as models for modern Gothic buildings. But after the erection of such striking examples of irregular domestic Gothic as Alexander Jackson Davis's baronial "Lyndhurst" (1838) at Tarrytown, civic and ecclesiastical architecture became more picturesque. Until 1844 the churches of Richard Upjohn, the leading ecclesiastical architect of the mid-century, are rigorously symmetrical, usually, as in New York's Trinity Church, with a tower placed in the center of the façade; but after that date Upjohn customarily disrupted the symmetrical arrangement by placing the tower at one of the corners.

The first great public building in the United States of full picturesque irregularity and asymmetry, James Renwick's Smithsonian Institution (1846), was Romanesque rather than Gothic, and a number of other early examples of asymmetrical civic architecture, including the city hall of Springfield, Massachusetts, and the Syracuse court house, were in the older Medieval mode.[2]

Another source of enthusiasm for the Gothic style was the belief that it was akin to the most characteristic and forceful works of romantic art, which burst from the orderly confines of classical form in quest of a never wholly attainable ideal. This conception of Gothic art originated with the German critics, Friedrich and August Wilhelm Schlegel. The Schlegels compared the works of great modern Christian writers such as Shakespeare, whom they called romantic, with Gothic buildings like Westminster Abbey and contrasted them to classical structures like the Pantheon as well as to the works of Sophocles. August Wilhelm conceived of Greek art and poetry as beautiful, perfect within clearly defined limits, and thought of Gothic and romantic works as infused with a spiritual striving for the infinite which could only be approximately achieved.[3] Friedrich Schlegel found similarity between Gothic architecture and Christian poetry in "the sublimity of the solitary idea which lies at the bottom of them all" and in the fact that "both in great measure remained ideal, and never [have] been brought to perfection in execution." [4]

Samuel Taylor Coleridge, the principal English disciple of the Schlegels, also conceived of the Gothic style as an architectural counterpart of romantic literature, not brought to material perfection but spiritual and ideal. He became interested in architecture rather late in life [5] but sometime before 1818 tried to wean Washington Allston from his love of classical architecture with the remark that "Grecian architecture is a thing but the Gothic is an idea." [6] In a series of lectures delivered in 1818 on the general character of the Gothic mind, Coleridge is reported to have said that Gothic art "entirely depended on a symbolical expression of the infinite,—which is not vastness, nor immensity, nor perfection, but whatever cannot be circumscribed, within the limits of actual sensuous being." [7]

A few years earlier, in a lecture on the "general characteristics of Shakespeare" which depended heavily on August Wilhelm Schlegel, Coleridge had stated

the Greeks reared a structure, which, in parts and as a whole, filled the mind with the calm and elevated impression of perfect beauty and symmetrical proportion. The moderns, blending materials, produced one striking whole. This may be illustrated by comparing the Pantheon with York Minster or Westminster Abbey. Upon the same scale we may compare Sophocles with Shakespeare: in one there is a completeness, a satisfying, an excellence on which the mind can rest; in the other we see a blended multitude of materials, great and little, magnificent and mean, mingled, if we may say so, with a dissatisfying, or falling short of perfection, yet so promising of our progression, that we would not exchange it for that repose of mind which dwells on the forms of symmetry in acquiesant admiration of grace.[8]

Two of the most interesting American statements of the Schlegel-Coleridge conception of Gothic form are found in travel books written by Nathaniel and Sophia Hawthorne. In *Our Old Home*, a book of English sketches, there is a remarkable description of a visit to Lichfield Cathedral. Hawthorne, a belated tourist sometimes startling in his obtuseness to works of art, is most perceptive in his response to the Gothic building. He writes that he became convinced that a Gothic cathedral is the greatest creative achievement of man because it is extremely "difficult to comprehend within one idea and yet [is] so consonant that it ultimately draws the beholder and his universe into its harmony." Hawthorne despaired of achieving the spiritual elevation of the Gothic and felt that "a flood of uncomprehended beauty" was sweeping down upon him of which he could grasp only the smallest portion. But he believed, despite his human inability to fully comprehend the Gothic, that he had derived something of value from his experience. "It was something gained, even to have that painful sense of . . . [his] own limitations, and that half-smothered yearning to soar beyond them." He concluded, "the cathedral showed me how earthly I was, but yet whispered deeply of immortality." [9]

Mrs. Hawthorne comparing Gothic with Greek architecture in her *Notes in England and Italy* pretty much equated the one with the intuitive, imaginative faculty which Coleridge called the reason and the other with the prosaic common-sense faculty he termed the understanding. She thought that the Greek style is "the clear, logical understanding, coming at truth mathematically by the way of reason" but that "the Gothic 'is of Imagination all compact,' 'in a fine frenzy rolling,' glancing from earth to heaven and heaven to earth—a crystallized poet, as it were, of endless variety, of scintillating fancy—soaring 'in immortal curves,' baffling geometric conclusions, setting known, established rules at defiance, wild beyond recognized art, flaming like fire, glowing like flowers and rainbows, soaring like birds, struggling for freedom, like a soul, never satisfied." It seemed to her that "a cathedral is really an image of the whole soul of man; and a Greek temple of his understanding only—of just decisions, serene, finished postulates, settled axioms." [10]

The qualities of the Gothic which bewildered, troubled, and entranced the Hawthornes, and which seemed to Mrs. Hawthorne to make it akin to the romantic imagination itself, go far in explaining the growing popularity of the style in the middle decades of the century. Of even greater significance in accounting for the appeal of Gothic architecture to a generation imbued with romanticism was the identification of the style with deified "nature."

The chief English spokesman of the developed romantic idea of nature, Wordsworth, culminates a century-long development, but his attitude differs strongly from his immediate predecessors of the picturesque school. The admirers of the picturesque loved the intricacy and variety of the countryside, but they looked at the natural landscape through the eyes of a painter, trying to compose it into pleasant scenes which were suitable for painting. Wordsworth, unlike these men, had no desire to impose an artistic order upon nature. Nature, in Wordsworth's opinion, could perform its function as the moral teacher of man only if the natural order was left in its original purity. Mankind should face nature, not critically with the idea of perfecting it, but receptively as a pupil, "in a wise passiveness." [11] "Our meddling intellect/ Misshapes the beauteous forms of things;/- We murder to dissect." [12]

The Wordsworthian conception of nature made slow progress at first in the United States. The only important American supporters of Wordsworth before 1820 were William Cullen Bryant and his friends on the *North American Review*, Willard Phillips and Richard Henry Dana.[13] The American transcendentalists were late in appreciating Wordsworth. It was not until the thirties that they saw him as one of the major figures of modern literature, and even then their praise was more for his "idea" than for his poetry.[14] They were ready for Wordsworth's idea because they had imbibed the Swedenborgian conception of nature as the guide and nurse of the soul from Sampson Reed's *Observations on the Growth of the Mind* which was published in Boston in 1826. Ten years after the appearance of Reed's pamphlet, Emerson published a thin volume on *Nature* which made the first important statement of the transcendentalist position. Nature, wrote Emerson, "is a remoter and inferior incarnation of God, a projection of God in the unconscious. But it differs from the body in one important respect. It is not, like that, now subjected to the human will. Its serene order is inviolable by us. It is, therefore, to us, the present expositor of the divine mind. It is a fixed point whereby we may measure our departure." [15] Thoreau as well as Emerson had a theory of nature akin to that of Wordsworth. In "The Natural History of Massachusetts" he stressed the spiritual refreshment provided by nature [16] and urged that none should undervalue the natural fact because "it will one day flower in a truth." [17]

The disciples of the picturesque demanded an architecture which was suited, because of irregularities of plan and elevation and form-destroying patterns of shadow and light, to a setting amidst natural scenery. But many naturalists of the Wordsworthian sort advocated a style which was believed to imitate natural forms instead of merely harmonizing with natural landscape.

From almost the beginning of the revival the Gothic style was associated with nature. The arboreal theory of the origin of the style made current in England by a note to Bishop William Warburton's edition of Pope in 1751 is symptomatic. Warburton, like others of his time, thought that Gothic architecture was actually the style of the Goths and wrote that this northern people devised it in Spain under the influence of their recollection of the groves in which they had worshiped in pagan times. He argued that when this source of Gothic architecture is taken into consideration the various peculiarities of the Gothic forms are accounted for. "For could the *Arches* be otherwise than pointed, when the workman was to imitate that curve which branches of two opposite trees make by their intersection with one another? Or could the *Columns* be otherways than split into distinct shafts, when they were to represent the Stems of a clump of trees?" Warburton went on to find a natural source for Gothic tracery in the branches and for stained glass in the leaves of the grove.[18]

Warburton's explanation of the beginning of the Gothic style became popular immediately and, although soon discredited by more careful students of the history of architecture, continued to appeal to romanticists interested in showing a connection between nature and art. Schelling adopted Warburton's theory half a century later and made the parallel even more elaborate. Bishop John Henry Hopkins, the author of the first American book on Gothic architecture, accepted the argument of Warburton but suggested that it was more reasonable to trace the style to palm trees rather than to an ordinary Medieval grove because ornaments derived from palms had decorated the temple of Solomon which he regarded as probably the original Gothic structure.[19] Emerson repeated, with minor variations, Warburton's explanation of the Gothic.[20] And eleven years later another American manifestation of the theory appeared in Samuel S. Cox's description of the cathedral of York, published in 1852, over a century after Warburton's note and many decades after it ceased to have any support from serious students of architecture.[21]

Analogies were frequently made between the forms of Gothic architecture and natural forms other than aisles of trees. One American traveller described the cathedral of Milan fancifully as "a flower-garden done in

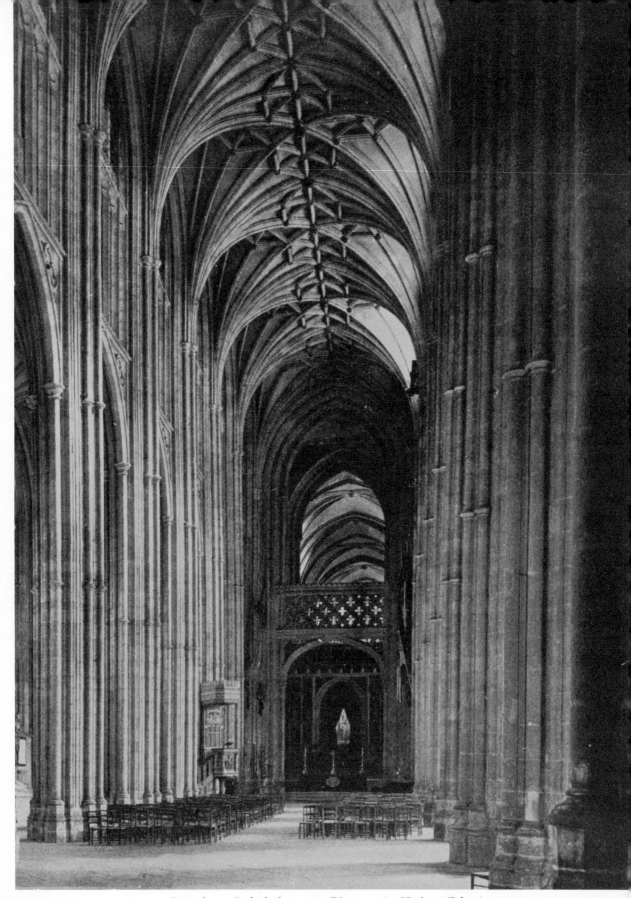

Canterbury Cathedral, nave. (Photograph, Herbert Felton)

Milan Cathedral. (Photograph, Brogi)

marble." [22] Two others compared the appearance of the exterior of that church, a Medieval structure notably congenial to nineteenth-century taste, to the effects of the frost.[23] Bayard Taylor wrote that the design of the building was reported to have been taken from Monte Rosa. In any case, he thought, the sculptured pinnacles which rose from all parts of the cathedral bore "a striking resemblance to the splintered ice crags of Savoy," showing how art "is in everything but the child of nature." [24] Henry VII's chapel in Westminster Abbey reminded John R. Tait of "the fretted interior of some grand cavern, where the stalactites, infinite in variety, possess a perfect unity of effect." [25]

More important than the theory that the Gothic style had originated in forest groves or the analogies made to specific natural forms was the identification of the style in a more general way with the organic processes of nature. Goethe and Friedrich Schlegel anticipated this interpretation,[26] but in the United States Ruskin's writings were the most influential source of the analogy between Gothic construction and natural processes. The immense vogue of Ruskin's books, which were more widely read in the United States than in England in the fifties and sixties,[27] was largely due to his essentially picturesque conception of esthetic form. But his ultimate contribution to architectural development was an ethical functionalism growing out of a love for natural beauty. The Wordsworthian source of much of Ruskin's thought is evident in his statement that "an architect should live as little in cities as a painter"; that he should be sent "to our hills, and let . . . study there what nature understands by a buttress, and what by a dome." [28] Although he realized that the vegetable theory of the origin of the Gothic was untenable, he was sympathetic toward it. The theory, Ruskin maintained, did suggest the character of mature Gothic because, while the style did not originate in an imitation of vegetation, it did develop into a resemblance to natural forms. The truth, he wrote, was even more impressive than the advocates of the old explanation supposed. "It was no chance suggestion of the form of an arch from the bending of a bough, but a gradual and continual discovery of a beauty in natural form which could be more and more perfectly transferred into those of stone, that influenced at once the heart of the people, and the form of the edifice." [29]

American writers also related Gothic architecture to organic growth. James Freeman Clarke, who compared the cathedral of Cologne in the process of completion, with new stones being placed beside weathered Medieval ones, to a wild forest "with young shoots and old trees side by side," was reminded by the Gothic of the immensity and prodigality of nature. "The unnecessary amount of space, the quantity of moulding and carving, the working of the stone into minute details, even high up where it can hardly be seen," he wrote, "makes these great works of art resemble the exuberance of nature, who never counts her leaves and flowers." [30] Horace B. Wallace, the American disciple of Auguste Comte, likened the Gothic method of construction to organic growth, writing that "Chartres or Ely is a tree, growing freely and boldly, encountering obstacles and surmounting or working them in with an energy that makes deviation a new and higher illustration of principle, exhibiting a thousand beauties of light and shade by its interlacing branches and its flowering foliage, glittering with dewy freshness, and full of the song of birds." [31]

After the 1830's, while the Gothic gradually gained favor, classical architecture lost ground. In the middle decades of the century when the Wordsworthian veneration of nature was almost universally prevalent, the classical styles were severely handicapped. The absolute regularity of classical buildings seemed unnatural and almost indecent. That is not the way of nature wrote Robert Dale Owen. "No leaf in the forest . . . is a servile copy of its fellow." [32] Sophia Hawthorne admired the variety of the Gothic arches of Lincoln Cathedral and was reminded of the system of nature with "no two leaves or flowers . . . precisely alike. Gothic sculpture and architecture . . . [she believed], represent and reproduce nature, and Grecian architecture seems to be art." [33] Her husband in describing the bell tower of the cathedral of Florence also exemplifies the romantic habit of identifying the Gothic style with nature and consequently disparaging classical art. He was struck by the "moral charm" of the minuteness of Gothic architecture "filling up its outline with a million beauties that perhaps may never be studied out by a single spectator." This he believed to be "the very process of nature. . . . Classical architecture [he wrote] is nothing but an outline, and affords no little points, no interstices where human feelings may cling and overgrow it like ivy." [34]

Hawthorne's phrase "moral charm" is indicative of the growing tendency to introduce ethical judgments into architectural criticism. When a divinized nature became the norm by which the various styles were measured, ethical issues were certain to be important in esthetic decisions. Ruskin is only the best known of the romantic art critics who fused, and at times confused, ethics and esthetics. Ethical issues were inextricably tied to esthetic ones in the functional theories which developed out of the naturalistic conception of Gothic architecture.

While the Gothic style never dominated American building in the middle

The Jayne Building, Philadelphia. Engraving by John M. Butler
courtesy of the Library Company of Philadelphia.

New York University. Engraving by Wade.

decades of the century, as had the Greek in the thirties, Gothic structures were numerous and their uses extremely varied. Classical architecture continued to be favored for public buildings but a number of court houses, city halls and the state capitols of Louisiana and Georgia were designed in the Gothic style. Perhaps its Medieval origin commended the Gothic to the Masonic order. In any case Gothic Masonic temples were erected in Philadelphia, New York, and Boston. John Haviland's Eastern State Penitentiary at Philadelphia of 1821–25 suggested the castellated Gothic to future designers of prisons. Railroad stations in Boston and Salem were also in the castellated manner and, although Gothic commercial structures were comparatively rare, Philadelphia's eight story Jayne Building of 1849 had a Venetian Gothic façade.

In domestic architecture the Antique styles continued to be used until mid-century, and in the cities the Renaissance manner became popular. The Italian villa and the free bracketed styles were the principal rivals of the Gothic in picturesque rural housing. Of the ten designs published in Downing's *Cottage Residences*, three were Italian, three were comparatively free of historical precedent, and four were at least loosely Gothic. The earliest Medieval design for an American college was submitted to Columbia by the elder James Renwick in 1814, but the first really influential one actually executed was for New York University at Washington Square in 1837 by Ithiel Town, Alexander Jackson Davis, James H. Dakin, and others. In 1842 both Harvard and Yale built libraries patterned after English Gothic chapels, and a few years later Davis produced a really comprehensive Gothic scheme for the Virginia Military Institute which served as the prototype for a number of castellated military schools.[35] Of course, the greatest triumph of the Gothic style was in ecclesiastical architecture. The preeminence of Gothic and other Medieval styles in American church design, which was established before the complete dissolution of the classical revivals, continued through the century, and then, though threatened, was not destroyed by the colonial revival.

Extensive and varied as the uses of mid-century Gothic became and delightful as were some of its nostalgic creations, it seems safe to say that the principal significance of the revival to architectural history lies in the revolutionary theories of structure which it engendered. Organic theories of central importance in modern architectural thought grew easily out of the conception of the Gothic style as a reflection of natural forms. Goethe, notable as a pre-Lamarckian, pre-Darwinian evolutionist, was among the first to conceive of the style as analogous to a natural organism with the various parts in fundamental relationship with each other. He described Strasbourg Cathedral as composed of "harmonious masses, animated by countless delicate details of structure . . . as in the works of eternal Nature, every form, down to the smallest fibril, alive, and everything contributing to the purpose of the whole!" [36] The two cardinal rules of A. Welby Pugin, foremost proponent of the Gothic style in England before Ruskin, are derived from a conception of the Gothic similar to Goethe's. Pugin declared that only features which contributed to its "convenience, construction, or propriety" should be incorporated in a building and that ornament should exist only to enrich the essential construction. His demand that the properties of natural materials be respected in architectural construction is related to the Wordsworthian "wise passiveness" before nature. He argued that "the construction itself should vary with the material employed, and the designs should be adapted to the material in which they are executed," and he thought that the Medieval architects were the first to follow these principles. They "turned the natural properties of the various materials to their full account, and made their mechanism a vehicle for their art." [37]

Pugin's ideas were taken up by Ruskin especially in the second of his lamps of architecture, "The Lamp of Truth." He traced the decline of Gothic architecture from the moment the emphasis shifted from the strips of tracery to the openings between them. Up to that time, he wrote, "the stone-work was necessarily considered, as it actually is, stiff and unyielding [but then] . . . it began to undulate like the threads of a cobweb lifted by the wind. It lost its essence as a structure of stone." Ruskin argued that this change sacrificed the principle of truth and the expression of the properties of the material and that it, in spite of charming effects achieved at first, was finally ruinous.[38]

The steep roofs customary in northern Gothic buildings were often cited by nineteenth-century writers as an example of the fusion of use and beauty in Gothic architecture. Pugin believed that the most esthetically pleasing pitch of a roof was one steep enough to shed snow easily but not so steep that it put too strong a perpendicular strain on the roof covering.[39] In a book published in Boston two years after the appearance of Pugin's volume, Edward Shaw located the source of the Gothic style in the steep roofs which were adopted for climatic reasons by the Saxon and Norman architects of the early Middle Ages. The later Midieval architects, wrote Shaw, were ready to take up any novelty "recommended by utility and beauty," and they developed the features of the mature Gothic from the hint provided by the functional roof. "It was soon seen that unbroken vertical lines and lofty buildings were necessary to harmonize with the high pitched roof; and the pointed arch is but a natural and easy deduction from these *data*." [40]

In the fifties American architectural writers began to show the influence of Ruskin's books. Horace B. Wallace maintained that Gothic decoration, of the best period, "is derived out of reality, and is representative of truth." The clustering of piers, he remarked, is not a fantastic play on circular form but an honest combination of separate shafts, and the magnificent rib-vaulting is merely a "display of the actual principles upon which the building is held up." [41] Henry Van Brunt, a young architect in the atelier of Richard Morris Hunt, declared to a meeting of the recently founded American Institute of Architects that the best periods of architecture were "those in which building material has been used with the most honest regard for its nature, attributes and capacities." He attributed the current admiration for buildings of the thirteenth century to a recognition in them of a complete alliance of nature's "innate powers with our adaptive skill in the production of objects of beautiful utility." In this high Gothic architecture nothing "makes us forget the quarry. The skill of the workman does not attempt to conceal or contradict the skill of God." Elaborating on Ruskin, he stated that the decline of the style began the moment that "the stone was taught to forget its native frown of power, its preadamite sternness, and was made to smile and flutter under the chisel." [42]

The pervasiveness of romantic functionalism based upon reverence for natural materials is shown by the frequent application to Greek architecture of functional explanations analogous to those devised for Gothic forms. These explanations usually were related to the Vitruvian theory that the form of the Doric temple originated in a wooden cottage.[43] Once this theory was accepted it was easy to see how the Doric ornamental system depended upon the methods of wooden construction, how "the decorative is directly founded upon the real, and retains that suggestion of nature and utility which gives it meaning and truth." [44] Samuel G. Ward stated that a man looking at a marble temple might, with justice, question the meaning of the details of the Doric order. "But," wrote Ward, "when he is told that this is a marble imitation of a wooden building, a reproduction in more costly material of a sacred historical form, he then sees in the triglyph the end of the wooden beam, with marks of the trickling water drops, in the metope the flat panel between." [45]

Organic theories, at first applied to Gothic and classical styles, eventually led to the conviction that no historical style could fully satisfy the demands of modern life. The insistence of romantic naturalists that the inherent qualities of natural materials be respected in architectural construction, that the various parts of a building be in organic relation to each other, and that the form of the whole grow out of its intended function culminated in a quest for a totally new type of architecture. A group of writers associated with Emerson were among the first to seek an architecture emancipated from historical precedents.[46] The belief that "nature is the symbol of spirit," that natural facts are "nouns of the intellect," "symbols of particular spiritual facts," and that "the feat of the imagination is in showing the convertibility of every thing into every other thing," [47] in accordance with the central Emersonian doctrine of correspondence, seemed to necessitate a kind of architecture that could not be contained within the framework of the traditional styles.

Emerson's theories of art and architecture follow logically from his theory of the correspondence of the facts of nature and those of the spirit. Because he considered nature the representative of the universal mind, the sole creator of the useful and the beautiful, he argued that "art must be a compliment to nature, strictly subsidiary." [48] To Emerson the role of the artist was to follow the lead of nature's forms rather than to impose an external, artificial order upon the natural one. "We feel, in seeing a noble building, which rhymes well, as we do in hearing a perfect song, that it is spiritually organic, that is, had a necessity in nature, for being, was one of the possible forms in the Divine mind, and is now discovered, and executed by the artist, not arbitrarily composed by him." [49]

The transcendentalist belief that natural facts would flower in truths led to a glorification of the raw materials of architecture.[50] Emerson felt that the organic esthetic called for a respectful use of wood, the common American building material, which, up to that time, had been regarded as merely a makeshift usable only when more worthy materials could not be afforded. "Hence our taste," he wrote, " . . . rejects paint, and all shifts, and shows the original grain of wood." [51] His friend, Samuel G. Ward, agreed with Emerson in considering the skillful use of materials according to their individual characteristics a prime source of beauty in architecture. He attacked the "would-be pretty buildings . . . [where] the material is entirely disguised, so that for aught we know they may be marble, or wood, or paste-board; all we see is a plain white surface." [52]

Related to the concern for materials was the belief that architectural expression should reflect the method of construction. Downing's argument that vertical boarding on the sides of houses expresses the main timbers of the wooden frame and therefore "signifies to the eye a wooden house," will be recalled. And he had continued, "the main weight of a stone or brick house is supported by walls laid in courses, and hence the truthfulness of showing horizontal courses in brick or stone buildings." [53] The writings of Gervase Wheeler, who emigrated from England in the forties, exemplify more clearly than those of Downing the application of the ethical functionalism of Pugin to wooden framed buildings.[54] Wheeler confessed his admiration for the principle of "reality" in Medieval architecture: "every form of even the simplest moulding; every line and portion of the building was contrived exactly to answer the purpose for which it was intended." He argued that modern architects should be guided by the principle of the Medieval builders instead of "servilely copying a bit here and there of their immortal works." [55] In Wheeler's view the application of the Gothic principle of expression of the materials and methods of construction had in the United States, where wood was the customary material for building, led to the creation of a "style of erection which may be considered as almost national." Wheeler described one of his designs, which Downing published in The Architecture of Country Houses, as "real," given character "by simplicity and fitness of construction." He explained that it was framed in such a way that the skeletal method of construction was expressed on the exterior. Heavy corner posts, mortised horizontal ties at the level of the springing of the roof, and vertical battens which held the boarding in place and suggested the studs of the frame were revealed externally, as was the framing of the roof.[56]

Beyond encouraging architectural expression of building materials and methods, the naturalism of Wordsworth, Bryant, and Emerson led to a fully functionalist esthetic based upon imitation of the natural processes themselves. One lesson which Emerson thought architects could learn from processes of nature was the inevitable connection between utility and beauty. O. S. Fowler, famous as the proponent of octagonal houses, agreed that utility and beauty are twins in all of nature which makes everything beautiful but "never puts on any thing exclusively for ornaments as such." [57] J. Elliott Cabot, friend of Emerson and translator of Schelling, demanded that the beauty of houses "grow as naturally from their use as the flower from its stem, so that it shall not be possible to say where the one ends and the other begins." [58] Emerson pointed to the multifold variations for utility apparent in the order of nature, writing that there are as many styles of architecture in nature "as creatures, or tenants, or reasons for erecting a building; a seashell, a bird's nest, a spider's web, a beaver's dam, . . . a cocoon, . . . a beehive, a lamprey's pyramid are examples. So a tree, so the shape of every animal, is the structure, the architecture, which Nature builds for a purpose, which rules the whole building and declares itself at sight." [59] And beauty in art, like beauty in nature, he believed, is attainable only by eliminating everything superfluous, by omitting all extraneous ornament, everything not originating in purpose. A beautiful building like the beautiful forms of nature was the result of rigorous submission to the law of function. In architecture as in poetry the artist must not impose an arbitrary structure of his own.

Thoreau agreed with Emerson that architectural ornaments should have "a necessity, and hence a beauty," and he stressed especially the need for organic unity in architecture. Our houses, he wrote, should be first "lined with beauty, where they come in contact with our lives, like the tenement of the shellfish and not overlaid with it." Architectural beauty must gradually grow from within outward, growing out of the character and needs of the inhabitant.[60]

The architectural writings of the neo-classic sculptor, Horatio Greenough, were the culmination in the United States of the functionalism that was based on romantic veneration for the natural world. Greenough urged American architects to turn from the imitation of admired historic models to the study of nature because "she will disclose a mine, richer than was ever dreamed of by the Greeks, in art as well as in philosophy." [61] Like Emerson and the others he was impressed by the union of beauty and function in growing things. Comparing the array of Solomon unfavorably with a lily in a field, he stated that "the lily is arrayed in heavenly beauty, because it is organized both in shape and color, to dose the germ of future lilies with atmospheric and solar influence." Greenough defined "Beauty as the promise of Function" and declared that normally beauty develops to completeness through action. He further remarked that decoration inevitably leads to more decoration and that, in his opinion, a decline in beauty sets in with the introduction of a single inorganic, non-functional thing either in shape or color.[62]

Greenough, like Thoreau,[63] believed that works of art must have an organic unity which began at the center and grew outward. "Let us begin from the heart as a nucleus," he wrote, "and work outwards. The most convenient size and arrangement of the rooms that are to constitute the building being fixed, the access of the light that may, of the air that must be wanted, being provided for, we have the skeleton of our building. Nay, we have all excepting the dress." [64] In a letter to Emerson, Greenough made the most concise statement of his conception of organic wholeness in architecture. Structure, he argued, should consist of "a scientific arrangement of spaces and forms to function and site . . . [with] an emphasis of features proportioned to their *graduated* importance in function . . . [and with] color and ornament to be decided and arranged and varied by strictly organic laws, having a distinct reason for each decision." [65]

Evidence that organic theories of architecture were not unique with Greenough or with the Emersonian circle but were formulated by others who were influenced by similar conceptions of nature yet favored traditional architectural forms, most often Medieval ones, appears in the theory of structure of Robert Dale Owen, social reformer, founder and chief critical supporter of the Romanesque Smithsonian Institution in Washington. Owen like Greenough argued that the planning of a building should "begin from within" and that the particular purposes required should be allowed "to block out its forms, to determine its inner proportions and decide the connection of its parts." And then, he wrote, the designer could "adjust and elaborate its architecture as its appropriate garb . . . in such guise, that the garment shall adapt itself to the individual form it is destined to clothe; fitting well, and displaying the peculiarities of that form to best advantage." [66]

Greenough was most pleased by such modern creations as bridges, fortifications, racing ships, and carriages in which he felt the designers had been freed from copying the past "by the stern organic requirements of the works." He pointed to the progress in ship design from the dugout canoe to the contemporary sloop-of-war and declared that "every advance in performance has been an advance in expression, in grace, in beauty, or grandeur." The modern sailing ship seemed to him vastly superior to any product of an academy of design, of connoisseurship, or of imitation of the Greeks because it was the result of man's study of the sea "where nature spoke

Smithsonian Institution, Washington, D.C., Lithograph by Sarony and Major
from Robert Dale Owen's Hints on Public Architecture.

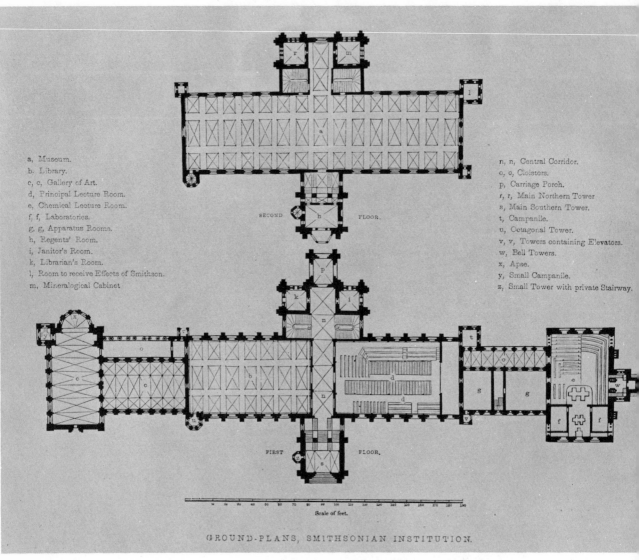

a, Museum.
b, Library.
c, c, Gallery of Art.
d, Principal Lecture Room.
e, Chemical Lecture Room.
f, f, Laboratories.
g, g, Apparatus Rooms.
h, Regents' Room.
i, Janitor's Room.
k, Librarian's Room.
l, Room to receive Effects of Smithson.
m, Mineralogical Cabinet

n, n, Central Corridor.
o, o, Cloisters.
p, Carriage Porch.
r, r, Main Northern Tower
s, Main Southern Tower.
t, Campanile.
u, Octagonal Tower.
v, v, Towers containing Elevators.
w, Bell Towers.
x, Apse.
y, Small Campanile.
z, Small Tower with private Stairway.

SECOND FLOOR.

FIRST FLOOR.

Scale of feet.

GROUND-PLANS, SMITHSONIAN INSTITUTION.

Smithsonian Institution, Washington, D.C. Plan.
From Robert Dale Owen's Hints on Public Architecture.

Yacht America. Lithograph by Currier & Ives.

Trotting wagon. Lithograph by Currier & Ives.

of the laws of building, not in the feather and in the flower, but in the winds and waves, and he bent all his mind to hear and obey." In the modern American trotting wagon Greenough saw the pretentious, old-fashioned coach transformed, as he thought the "old-fashioned palatial display" in building should be transformed in this country, with "the redundant . . . pared down . . . [and] the superfluous dropped . . . [and with] the necessary itself reduced to its simplest expression." The design of the carriage like that of the ship reflected a respect for natural things. "The slender harness and tall gaunt wheels are not only effective, they are beautiful —for they respect the beauty of the horse, and do not uselessly task him." [67]

The naturalism of Emerson led easily enough to an organic theory of architecture stressing respect for natural materials and urging the essential identity of beauty and utility. But the functional arguments of Greenough are notable among others of their time for the frequent analogies drawn between animal and architectural structure. As a sculptor Greenough made a thorough study of comparative anatomy. And, like the functionalism of Louis Sullivan and Frank Lloyd Wright which drew support from Darwinian evolutionary theories, the functionalism of Greenough developed from the study of the way animal organisms were adapted to their particular functions. [68] In arguing against limiting freedom of design by using traditional models of form or arbitrary laws of proportion, he pointed to the tremendous variety apparent in the skins and skeletons of animals. And he cited as examples of the adaption of natural forms to functions "the length of the vertebrae of the neck in grazing quadrupeds increased, so as to bring the incisors to the grass . . . the vertebrae shortened in beasts of prey, in order to enable the brute to bear away his victim . . . the wading birds on stilts, the strictly aquatic birds with paddles . . . [and the general use of] color arrayed either for disguise or aggression." The eagle, the lion, and the greyhound were cited to illustrate the way in which nature fused functionally adapted parts into unified organic wholes. When you see an eagle, wrote Greenough, "carry in your mind the proportions and lines of the dove, and mark how the finger of God, has by the mere variation of diameters, converted the type of meekness into the most expressive symbol of majesty. . . . Whence the beauty and majesty of the bird? It is the oneness of his function that gives him his grandeur, it is transcendental mechanism alone that begets his beauty." [69]

Functional necessity and not arbitrary proportions, argued Greenough, should be the basis of architectural as well as animal organization. The fundamental law of architecture which is at the basis of all styles is that the size and forms of structures be adapted "to the climate they are exposed to, and the offices for which they are intended," with their ornaments in harmony "with the nature that they embellished, and the institutions from which they sprang." [70]

The functional theories of architecture which grew out of the romantic reverence for nature foreshadow the central rationale of the modern movement. If the organic theories of Greenough drew support from study of natural organisms, several modern functionalists were influenced by Darwinism. The growing strength of functional theories in architecture hastened the eventual doom of the various traditional styles. Supporters of Gothic or classical architecture might argue that their favorite style was more suited to modern American use than any other historical style, but they were unable to compete on functional grounds with the proponents of a new architecture designed especially for modern needs. And, as Vincent Scully has well demonstrated, the final triumph of the modern style in the United States was anticipated by a school of wooden domestic architecture which developed from Downing's and Wheeler's application of ethical functionalism to frame construction. Architects of what Scully calls the "stick style" gave increasingly dramatic expression to the elements of the frame so that houses resembled "an interwoven basketry of sticks." Together with the expression of the frame came a general loosening of interior spatial arrangement and a growing emancipation from traditional styling. Full maturity of this architecture, which was shaped by both the picturesque esthetic and romantic functionalism, came in the great shingled houses of the eighties.[71]

Notes

1. *Inquiry into the Origin of Our Ideas of the Sublime and Beautiful*, 150, 156–158.

2. A notable early example of asymmetrical massing in a public building was Henry Austin's railroad station in New Haven which combined Italian villa, Chinese, and Indian motifs. The plan of this building was as ordered and symmetrical as the exterior elevation was bizarre. Cf. Meeks, *The Railroad Station*, 52–54.

3. A. W. Schlegel, *A Course of Lectures on Dramatic Art and Literature* (London, 1871), 23, 27. These lectures were delivered in Vienna in 1808 and published in 1809–11.

4. *Lectures on the History of Literature* (Philadelphia, 1818), 335. These lectures were delivered in Vienna in 1812.

5. See notes to J. Shawcross's edition of the *Biographia Literaria* (London: Oxford University Press, 1949), II, 312–313.

6. Jared B. Flagg, *The Life and Letters of Washington Allston* (New York, 1892), 65–66.

7. Notes by Joseph H. Green, printed by Thomas M. Raysor in *Coleridge's Miscellaneous Criticism* (Cambridge: Harvard University Press, 1936), 7.

8. *Coleridge's Shakespearian Criticism*, T. M. Raysor, ed. (Cambridge, 1930), II, 262–263.

9. (Boston and New York, 1899), 153–154; cf. Coleridge, notes of William Hammond in Raysor, *op. cit.,* 11–12.

10. (New York, 1869), 82–83. Mrs. Hawthorne's book was not published until 1869, but it was based on travel notes made in 1857. Mrs. Hawthorne does not follow Coleridge's terminology strictly but her dichotomy certainly reflects thinking similar to his.

11. "Expostulation and Reply," line 24.

12. "The Tables Turned," lines 25–28.

13. William Charvat, *The Origins of American Critical Thought* (Philadelphia: University of Pennsylvania Press, 1936), 73.

14. Perry Miller, *The Transcendentalists* (Cambridge: Harvard University Press, 1950), 97–98. Cf. Orestes A. Brownson, "The Poetical Works of William Wordsworth," *The Boston Quarterly Review*, vol. II, no. 2 (1839), 160, and Ralph Waldo Emerson, "Thoughts on Modern Literature," *The Dial*, vol. I, no. 2 (1840), 150; these passages are reprinted in *The Transcendentalists* on pages 435 and 97 respectively.

15. *Nature* in *The Complete Essays and Other Writings of Ralph Waldo Emerson* (New York: Modern Library, 1940), 36.

16. See Carl Bode, *The Portable Thoreau* (New York: Viking Press, 1947), 33–34. This essay was printed originally in *The Dial*, vol. III, no. 1 (1842), 19–40.

17. In Bode, *op. cit.,* 56.

18. *The Works of Alexander Pope*, III (London, 1760 edition), 328–329. William Stukeley anticipated Warburton by a quarter of a century, writing in his *Itinerarium Curiosum* that the "idea" of Gothic architecture "is taken from a walk of trees, whose touching heads are curiously imitated by the roof" ([London, 1724], 64), cited by Arthur O. Lovejoy, "The First Gothic Revival and the Return to Nature," *Essays in the History of Ideas* (Baltimore: Johns Hopkins Press, 1948), 153.

19. *Essay on Gothic Architecture* (Burlington, Vermont, 1836), 2–3, fn. 6.

20. "Thoughts on Art," *The Dial*, vol. I, no. 3 (1841), 376.

21. *A Buckeye Abroad* (New York, 1852), 409.

22. Theodore B. Witmer, *Wild Oats, Sown Abroad* (Philadelphia, 1853), 199.

23. N. P. Willis, *Pencillings by the Way* (second edition; London, 1842), 324; Bayard Taylor, *Views A-Foot* (first edition, 1846; New York, 1854), 242.

24. *Ibid.,* 243. W. C. Dana also compared the cathedral to a mountain, *A Transatlantic Tour* (New York, 1853), 297.

25. *European Life, Legend, and Landscape* (Philadelphia, 1859), 39.

26. Goethe's essay on Strasbourg Cathedral in Joel E. Spingarn's *Goethe's Literary Essays* (New York, 1921), 8, and Schlegel's *Principles of Gothic Architecture*, printed in *The Aesthetic and Miscellaneous Works* (London, 1849), 56.

27. According to R. H. Wilenski six years passed before there was a second English edition of *The Seven Lamps of Architecture* and then the book was out of print for twenty years; it took seven years to exhaust the first edition of the opening volume of *The Stones of Venice* and fourteen for the first editions of the other two volumes; there was no complete reprinting until the seventies, *John Ruskin* (London, 1933), 370. H. R. Hitchcock lists American editions of *The Seven Lamps* in 1849 (the year of the first London edition), 1852, 1854, 1857, 1859, 1863, 1866, and 1868, and an edition of volume I of *Stones of Venice* in 1851 (the same year as the London first) and editions of all three volumes in 1860, 1864, 1865, and 1867, *American Architectural Books*, 88–90.

28. *The Seven Lamps of Architecture* (New York: Thomas Y. Crowell, n.d., reprinted from the sixth English edition), 133.

29. *The Stones of Venice*, II (Everyman's ed.; London and New York, n.d.), 184. The Gothic use of ornament derived from natural things arranged in accordance with

their role in nature pleased Ruskin greatly; the Corinthian capital with its acanthus leaves was his favorite among the classical capitals, *Seven Lamps of Architecture,* 149.

30. *Eleven Weeks in Europe* (Boston, 1852), 59, 244.

31. *Art, Scenery and Philosophy in Europe* (Philadelphia, 1855), 77.

32. *Hints on Public Architecture* (New York, 1849), 67.

33. *Notes in England and Italy,* 35.

34. *Passages from the French and Italian Notebooks* (Boston and New York, 1899), 400.

35. Newton, *Town and Davis,* 229, 290–291.

36. In Springarn, *op. cit.,* 8.

37. *The True Principles of Pointed or Christian Architecture* (London, 1841), 1–2.

38. *Seven Lamps of Architecture,* 77–81.

39. *Op. cit.,* 11.

40. *Rural Architecture* (Boston, 1843), 42–43.

41. *Op. cit.,* 84–86. See also Wheeler, *Rural Homes,* 32.

42. "Cast Iron in Decorative Architecture," *The Crayon,* vol. VI, no. 1 (1859), 15.

43. This theory had been elaborated on by writers in the classical tradition like Quatremère de Quincy. And neo-classical theorists such as Carlo Lodoli, the Abbé Laugier, and the architect, C. N. Ledoux, had advocated functionalism in the eighteenth century.

44. H. B. Wallace, *op. cit.,* 82–83; see also R. W. Emerson, "Thoughts on Art," *loc. cit.,* 376.

45. "Notes on Art and Architecture," *The Dial,* vol. IV, no. 1 (1843), 109.

46. See Robert B. Shaffer, "Emerson and his Circle: Advocates of Functionalism," *Journal of the Society of Architectural Historians,* vol. VII, nos. 3–4 (1948), 17–20.

47. Emerson, "Nature," *loc. cit.,* 14; "Beauty" in *Conduct of Life* (Boston and New York: Houghton Mifflin, Standard Library Edition, n.d.), 288.

48. "Thoughts on Art," *loc. cit.,* 368–369; see also the later version of this essay, "Art," in *Society and Solitude* (Boston and New York: Houghton Mifflin, Standard Library Edition, n.d.), 44. This passage refers to "useful art" but Emerson also argued that art which aims primarily at beauty rather than utility should be "subordinated to Ideal Nature . . . so that it shall be the production of the universal soul," "Thoughts on Art," *loc. cit.,* 373, and "Art," *loc. cit.,* 51.

49. "Thoughts on Art," *loc. cit.,* 375.

50. Donald D. Egbert has shown how under the influence of evolutionary ideas modern functionalist theories of architecture have stressed the importance of expressing the intrinsic qualities of natural materials. He writes that "the functionalist tends to believe that nature, man, and God (if any) are all one" and "because the functionalist . . . tends to hold that reality lies in the phenomena of nature . . . he . . . in architecture . . . correspondingly tends to give expression to the natural qualities of materials as ends in themselves"—"The Idea of Organic Expression and American Architecture" in *Evolutionary Thought in America,* edited by Stow Persons (New Haven: Yale University Press, 1950), 344–345.

51. "Beauty," *loc. cit.,* 276.

52. "Notes of Art and Architecture," *loc. cit.,* 110.

53. *The Architecture of Country Houses,* 52.

54. For Scully's perceptive account of Wheeler, upon which my discussion is based, see "Romantic Rationalism and the Expression of Structure in Wood," *loc. cit.,* 135–138.

55. *Rural Homes,* 31–32.

56. Quoted by Downing in *The Architecture of Country Houses,* 298, 300–302.

57. *A Home for All* (New York, 1851), 6, 22. Fowler wrote that after wondering about the lack of progress in architecture he asked himself, "Why not take our pattern from NATURE. Her forms are mostly SPHERICAL. She had ten thousand globular or cylindrical forms to one square one. . . . Why not, then, adopt this spherical form for houses? It is adopted in fruits, eggs, grain, etc., so as to enclose the greatest amount in the smallest compass, and also to secure them against injuries. What should we think of a square apple or a right-angled egg?"

58. "Notes on Domestic Architecture," *Atlantic Monthly,* vol. I, no. 3 (1858), 262–263.

59. *Journals of Ralph Waldo Emerson*, IX (Boston and New York, 1913), 323. See also Leopold Eidlitz, "On Style," *The Crayon*, vol. V, no. 5 (1858), 140–141.

60. *Walden* (Boston and New York, 1894), 65, 75, 76.

61. "American Architecture" in *A Memorial of Horatio Greenough*, edited by Henry T. Tuckerman (New York, 1853), 121–122. This essay first appeared in *United States Magazine and Democratic Review*, vol. XIII, no. 62 (1843), 206–210. For discussions of Greenough see F. O. Matthiessen, *American Renaissance* (New York: Oxford University Press, 1941), 136, 140–154, and Egbert, "The Idea of Organic Expression and American Architecture," *loc. cit.*, 366. Van Wyck Brooks called attention to Greenough in *The Flowering of New England* (New York: E. P. Dutton, 1936), 450–453.

62. "Relative and Independent Beauty," in *A Memorial of Horatio Greenough*, 132–136. The material collected by Tuckerman was published by Greenough under the pseudonym Horace Bender in *The Travels, Observations and Experiences of a Yankee Stonecutter* (New York, 1852).

63. Thoreau was introduced to Greenough's theories by Emerson, but he rejected them as "little better than the common dilettantism"—*Walden*, 75. Matthiessen attributes Thoreau's blindness to the similarity between Greenough's ideas and his own to Thoreau's need at this time to reject anything recommended by Emerson; *op. cit.*, 153–154.

64. "American Architecture," *loc. cit.*, 125.

65. Emerson included an excerpt from this letter in *English Traits* (Boston and New York, 1903), 6.

66. *Op. cit.*, 44. There is however a far greater dichotomy between the essentially symmetrical plan and the highly picturesque exterior of Renwick's Smithsonian building than Owen's theory would lead his reader to expect.

67. "Structure and Organization," *A Memorial of Horatio Greenough*, 173, 176–177, 181–182; "American Architecture," *loc. cit.*, 124–125; "Aesthetics at Washington," *A Memorial to Horatio Greenough*, 78. Both Emerson and Greenough's patron, Fenimore Cooper, were fascinated by American practical design. Emerson noted in his journal for 1847 that "the modern architecture is ship building"—VII (Boston and New York, 1912), 333. Cooper wrote that "the only people in Europe who have a respectful opinion of the Americans are those who see their ships"—*Excursions in Italy* (Paris, 1838), 33. Cooper praised American axes and thought American plows "more beautiful, graceful, and convenient" than any which "are probably to be found in the whole of Europe united." In this fact, he wrote, is the germ of American greatness—*Notions of the Americans*, II (Philadelphia, 1832), 115; cited by Matthiessen, *op. cit.*, 145.

68. Egbert believes that Greenough was influenced by evolutionary ideas, "The Idea of Organic Expression and American Architecture," *loc. cit.*, 366. On the other hand it is possible that Greenough was unaffected by pre-Darwinian evolutionary theories and simply accepted the ideas of natural teleology current in the early nineteenth century. In any case an interest in comparative anatomy was shown as early as Greenough's sophomore year at Harvard; Nathalia Wright, "Horatio Greenough's Borrowings from the Harvard College Library," *Harvard Library Bulletin*, vol. IX, no. 3 (1955), 406–410.

69. "Structure and Organization," *loc. cit.*, 174–175.

70. "American Architecture," *loc. cit.*, 129.

71. Scully, "Romantic Rationalism and the Expression of Structure in Wood," *loc. cit.* and *The Shingle Style* (New Haven: Yale University Press, 1955).

4

The Gothic as a Style
for Protestantism

THE EXTENDED STRUGGLE OVER THE PROPRIETY OF GOTHIC ARCHITECTURE FOR Protestant worship is one of the most interesting episodes in nineteenth-century American architecture. The advocates of the Gothic were faced with a vigorous hostility to any appeal to the senses in houses of worship and a frequent identification of the Medieval styles with the detested ceremonies of Catholicism.

Two main traditions in ecclesiastical architecture had taken form in the seventeenth century. In the South and, for the most part, in the Middle Colonies the early Anglican churches followed English Gothic models. The first permanent church at Jamestown, the second Parish Church at Williamsburg, and the surviving Newport Parish, or St. Luke's, Church of Smithfield, Virginia (1632) were colonial recollections of the Gothic parish churches of the mother country. All were fronted by massive square towers and had buttresses along their walls. Rudimentary brick tracery appears in the pointed windows of the Newport Parish Church. By the eighteenth century Gothic reminiscences became increasingly rare, and in the second and third decades Anglican churches in the Colonies began to be patterned after the type Christopher Wren had designed to replace the Medieval churches lost in the great London fire of 1666. Wren's baroque spires became so thoroughly

St. Luke's Church, Smithfield, Va., Photograph by Robert A. Flournoy,
Virginia Chamber of Commerce.

Christ Church, Philadelphia. (Photograph by Frank Cousins, Essex Institute, Salem, Mass.)

naturalized that they seemed essential features of the coast from northern New England to Charleston.

Fully as significant for the development of American ecclesiastical architecture as the Anglican effort to naturalize the English parish church was the attempt of New England Puritans to create a simple and ascetic church architecture unlike anything in the European tradition. The earliest Puritan "meeting houses" were simply houses used for meeting; they were used for secular as well as religious meetings and were in no way differentiated externally from ordinary houses. Later meeting houses became larger and more distinctive, but they retained their spare and secular character. The only remaining seventeenth-century religious building in New England, the Old Ship Meeting House in Hingham, Massachusetts (1681), is nearly square in plan with bare clapboarded walls, a hipped roof and a simple belfry at the top. The pulpit is placed in the middle of one of the longer sides and the pews are arranged facing it. A similar auditorium plan was used in Boston as late as 1729 for the Old South Meeting House, which was clothed with a Wren type exterior.

The continuing influence of the old distrust of anything in church furnishings that might excite the senses is revealed in Americans as diverse as John Adams and Samuel F. B. Morse. Adams visited a "Romish chapel" on his first trip to Philadelphia for the Continental Congress in the fall of 1774 and found "the scenery and music so calculated to take in mankind" that he wondered how the Reformation ever succeeded.[1] Morse showed a similar attraction to, and fear of, sensuousness in religious ceremonies while visiting the Cathedral of Milan over half a century later. He found the Catholic system of worship "admirably contrived" to grasp the imagination of the participants. "All the arts of the imagination," he wrote, "are pressed into its service; architecture, painting, sculpture, music have lent all their charm to enchant the senses and impose on the understanding by substituting for the solemn truths of God's Word, which are addressed to the understanding, the fictions of poetry and the delusions of feeling." [2]

In view of the widespread suspicion of religious structures and ceremonies that excited the senses and feelings, a surprising number of Gothic buildings were erected for various Protestant sects in the early decades of the nineteenth century.[3] But most of these were simple rectangular structures of stone or wood, decorated with varying amounts of more or less correct Gothic ornament but without the structural and spatial complexity of the true Gothic. Only a few attempts were made to rationalize the adoption of the Gothic

Old Ship Meeting House, Hingham, Mass. (Photograph, H. Wickliffe Rose from
The Colonial Houses of Worship in America, **Hastings House, Publishers)**

**Old Ship Meeting House, Hingham, Mass., interior. (Photograph, H. Wickliffe Rose from
The Colonial Houses of Worship in America, Hastings House, Publishers)**

style for Protestantism,[4] and most of the "carpenters' Gothic" churches adhered fully as well as their neighbors of the Wren type to the traditional Protestant ideal for religious structures expressed by Asher Benjamin when he wrote in 1832 that a church should be designed so as to produce "serious and devotional feelings" in the worshippers. This, he thought, could best be done by composing the structure "of large, bold, angular outlines" with unbroken cornices and entablatures over the columns, and by "giving all the decorations . . . a large and grave appearance; excluding all ornaments composed of slender, curved, or winding outlines, which are expressive of lightness and gayety." He recommended large windows but warned against the effects of too glaring light and gay and bright colors, which he considered to be "opposed to solemnity in a house of worship." [5]

As might have been expected from its ritualistic character and its roots in a medieval English past, the Episcopal church led the battle for the use of Gothic architecture. As early as 1807 the Episcopalian *Churchman's Magazine* of New Haven described Gothic solemnity as more fitting for religious exercises than "the more light and finical . . . [style] of Greece." [6] Similar feelings were expressed at the time of the erection of Ithiel Town's Trinity Church in New Haven in 1814.[7] As American Gothic churches gradually lost the severe rectangularity of the meeting house and assumed a somewhat more archeologically correct Gothic form, Episcopalians continued to lead the way. Among the important Episcopal churches designed in the twenties were St. Stephen's in Philadelphia (1822–23), Christ Church in Hartford (1827–29), and Trinity in Boston (1828–29).

John Henry Hopkins, Bishop of Vermont, wrote for his fellow clergymen the earliest American book devoted to the Gothic. In 1823 Hopkins had turned from the law to become rector of struggling Trinity Church in Pittsburgh. He reinvigorated the parish and designed a new church building in the Gothic style. After a few years he moved on to Trinity Church in Boston, and then went, as first Bishop of Vermont, to Burlington, where his *Essay on Gothic Architecture* was published in 1836. Years later he became Presiding Bishop and played a key role in reuniting the church after the Civil War.

Known primarily as a student of patristic writings, Hopkins was associated with the powerful high church party of Bishop Hobart, whose views anticipated in some respects those of the Oxford Movement. In the United States as in England, the high churchmen took the lead in urging the adoption of the Gothic style for church buildings. The high church party of the Episcopal church shared in the general nineteenth-century movement toward a more emotional conception of religion, and in the Gothic the party found a style ideally adapted to its stress upon both liturgy and emotion.

A conservative Calvinist like Theodore Dwight, Jr., might reject the style as alien to American traditions because it influenced the feelings "independently of the judgment" and obscured "the objects and ends of our creation," [8] but the very qualities which repelled Dwight made Gothic architecture seem to Bishop Hopkins particularly appropriate for religious use. To him it seemed sublime and he loved its indefiniteness, its lack of clear, bold, angular outlines. He delighted in the vertical lines of the Gothic, which unlike the horizontal lines of classical architecture, seemed fitted "by an easy correspondence, to the offices of that blessed religion, which takes the heart from the contemplation of earth, and directs it to its heavenly inheritance." The multiplication of vertical lines in the buttresses, pinnacles, mullioned windows, and in the clustered shafts of the piers served "to lead the eye of the beholder upwards; causing, by a kind of physical association, an impression of sublimity more exalted than any other sort of architecture can produce." Hopkins objected to the customary American system of lighting churches, arguing that only enough light should be admitted to allow reading in comfort because any more than this "destroys solemnity, and is unfriendly to devotion." Stained glass for church windows suited him exactly; it not only moderated the light but also produced "a rich, mellow, and solemn effect." [9]

It would be a mistake to attribute the popularity of the Gothic style among Episcopalians entirely to the championship of men like the scholarly Hopkins. The diary of Philip Hone suggests that snobbery and fashion contributed to its vogue. Hone tells of Renwick's unfinished Grace Church on Broadway, where pew rent was to run as high as three dollars a Sunday, being visited by fashionable parties after services had ended in other churches. Then the uncompleted interior was filled with ladies in feathers and mousseline-de-laine and dandies with mustaches and high-heeled boots and the lofty arches resounded "with astute criticisms upon *Gothic Architecture* from fair ladies who . . . had the advantages of foreign travel, and scientific remarks upon acoustics from elderly millionaires who . . . [did] not hear quite so well as formerly." [10]

Not all Protestants in the forties were able to accept the Gothic as easily as did high church Episcopalians. Although the belief was common that the original Protestant austerity in places of worship had been too extreme, suspicion of the Gothic continued because of its Roman Catholic past, and opposition to the style on religious grounds endured beyond the middle of the

Grace Church, New York. Lithograph by Ackerman,
the Edward W. C. Arnold Collection lent by the Metropolitan Museum of Art.
(Photograph, courtesy of the Museum of the City of New York)

century. In 1843 the Reverend Edward N. Kirk, a Princeton-educated Congregationalist who considered music to be the only art sanctioned for religious services by the New Testament, declared himself opposed to the Gothic because it originated in times "when a false philosophy, aided by a corrupted Christianity, and despotism in Church and State, had fettered and stifled the soul." [11] Nine years later Henry P. Tappan echoed Kirk's anti-authoritarian blast at Gothic churches writing that "a Gothic building is kingly, proud, stern, awful" whether, as in the fortified castle, it expresses the power of the baron or, as in the church, it expresses "the absolutism of the priest." Unlike the Greek temple, he continued, the Gothic cathedral has no connection with intellectual liberty; "dreams of tyranny haunt its solemn aisles." [12]

Although all out attacks on the Gothic continued to be made, they became increasingly rare. After the late forties opponents of the style were apt to stress the practical difficulties involved in adapting it to Protestant services rather than to attack it for its essential qualities or its historic association with Roman Catholicism. Describing the Church of the Saviour, a recently constructed Gothic church for Boston Unitarians, in the *Christian Examiner* in 1850, Thomas C. Clarke wrote that architecturally speaking the structure was a gem and, if it had been designed for Catholic worship, a flawless one. He remarked that Gothic cathedrals were perfectly suited to Catholic services. "The 'long-drawn aisles' and interminable vistas were intended to give vast processions of worshippers opportunity of seeing the elevation of the host and the splendid ceremonies of the mass. The 'fretted vaults' resounded with the music of the majestic organ, and the mingled anthems of a thousand voices. The 'garish light of day' was excluded by the rich stained glass of the windows, and replaced by a dim, religious twilight, which aided the solemn effect of the scene. Everything was calculated to stimulate emotion and repress thought."

There were, however, he thought, insurmountable difficulties which blocked all attempts to make Gothic architecture really suitable for the Congregational type of worship. In a Protestant church which retains the essential Gothic features, "the preacher can hardly be seen at the end of one of the long aisles, and had he the voice of Stentor, he could hardly hope to penetrate the forest of columns and projections which intercept sight and sound." He protested that stained glass usually made it so dark that it was difficult to read hymn books and remarked that if the sun did happen to be strong the colors made the congregation look like a group of "disabled prize fighters, astonishing the beholders with green spots on the roseate bonnets of the ladies, and purple patches on the 'frosty pows' of the elders." In conclusion Clarke stated that the "eminently social" Protestant worship of the congregational type requires buildings which are "light, airy, and cheerful." [13]

In reply to the attacks upon the Gothic as an ecclesiastical style for Protestantism, partisans of the style frequently followed the strategy of the great Catholic Gothicist, Pugin, and emphasized the pagan background of classical architecture.[14] The young Arthur D. Gilman, later to be an important architect in Boston and New York, in answering in 1843 Kirk's attack upon the Gothic style, quoted Pugin with approval and expressed a sharp distaste for the "monomanic admirers of Stuart's Athens" who have already taken over "our banks and our breweries, our taverns and tanneries . . . everything, in short, from an exchange down to a hen-coop" and are now "staking out the ground plan of the house of God on the model of a heathen temple, and overlaying the shrine of Christian worship with the senseless emblems of heathen sacrifice." [15] Another, also arguing against Kirk, declared that Greek architecture is "indelibly associated with a most sensual and voluptuous mythology; while the Gothic, however dark and barbarous may have been [the period of its beginnings], sprang into light and flourished and had its chief glory under christian auspices, was used for christian purposes, and its purest models are those prepared for the worship of the Living God." [16]

An ingenious, if dubious, variation of Pugin's argument was advanced by J. Coleman Hart and N. H. Chamberlain who claimed the Gothic style for Protestantism and identified the "pagan" styles of the Renaissance with the church of Rome. Hart told the American Institute of Architects that Christianity developed Gothic architecture which remained its style until "superstitions or errors grew rife . . . [In the doctrines of the church and] architecture, like her parent became corrupted." [17] Chamberlain, like Hart, glossed over the Catholic past of Gothic architecture and tried to identify the classical styles with the Roman church. He also anticipated later nineteenth-century Pan-Germanism, maintaining that the Gothic is the style of the Middle Ages, the epoch of Teutonism, and therefore belongs to American Protestants because of their Teutonic past.[18]

Generally speaking, the most striking effect of romanticism upon religion was to reassert the importance of the emotions. Protestantism had from the beginning been suspicious of any hint of sensuousness in religious services, and in the late eighteenth century America, partly in reaction to the disturbances of the Great Awakening, a distrust of emotionalism in religion became

prevalent. Deism and Unitarianism were perhaps the most notable manifestations of a cool rationalism which affected much of Protestantism. But
with the development of romanticism with its insistence upon the primacy
of feeling and of the supra-rational powers of the mind, most Protestants,
Transcendentalists as well as conservative high-church Episcopalians, turned
against rationalism.

Among the results of the new attitude towards emotionalism in religion was
a smoothing the way for more widespread adoption of the Gothic architecture for all types of Protestant worship. It now became easier for others than
Roman Catholics and high-church Episcopalians to adopt the style for church
buildings. Protestants came to prefer the Gothic for the very reasons that their
ancestors had suspected it. Typical of the changing attitude toward emotional experiences in religion was an argument made in support of the Gothic
in the controversy which ran in the *Boston Daily Advertiser* in 1843. Specifically attacking the anti-sensuous point of view of Edward N. Kirk, the
writer, stated that all churches must, through their forms and colors, make
some impression upon the senses and argued that every effort should be made
to direct such sense impressions to religious purposes. He wrote that in pagan
philosophy there was an oscillation between "attempts to destroy or neutralize
the senses, and the license which naturally follows defeated severity," but
that Christianity "taught the possibility and duty of a sanctified life of all
the senses, as the intention of our creator, rather than self-inflicted blindness,
deafness and mutilation." He regarded as nonsense the old Protestant asceticism which denied "that form, color and sound shall ever contribute aught
toward the worship of God who made them all." [19]

In the thirties such a staunch Unitarian as Orville Dewey might express a
careful preference for Gothic architecture,[20] but in the fifties the idea that
the Gothic was the best, indeed the only, style for churches swept most of
Protestantism before it. The customary identification of Gothic architecture
with nature, at a time when nature was regarded as more than half divine,
helped to make the style seem especially suited for church buildings. But of
even greater importance was the growing conviction that the Gothic was
uniquely suited to express the religious spirit.

About 1850, Downing threw his influence behind the Gothic as an ecclesiastical style with an argument which recalled Bishop Hopkins. He wrote
that in classical architecture the leading idea is embodied in the horizontal,
in the level cornice which constitutes "the 'level line of rationality,' " and
makes the Greek style fitted for lecture rooms, town halls, legislative and

scientific assemblies and "for all civil purposes where the reason of man is supreme." But the dominating idea of the Gothic style, its aspiring vertical lines, is particularly congenial to religious feelings. "Upward, higher and higher, it soars, lifting everything, even ponderous stones, poising them in the air in vaulted ceilings or piling them upwards towards Heaven, in spires and steeples and towers, that, in the great cathedrals, almost seem to pierce the sky. It must be a dull soul that does not catch and feel something of this upward tendency . . . as well as its subdued and mellow light, and its suggestive and beautiful forms." [21] (See illustration, page 120.)

A few years later a paper read to the American Institute of Architects by Leopold Eidlitz went beyond Downing in defining the appeal of Gothic forms for the religious sensibility of mid-century. Eidlitz, born in Prague and educated in Vienna, worked briefly for Richard Upjohn, later designed a number of important Gothic churches and commercial buildings and was also responsible for Iranistan, P. T. Barnum's famed Saracenic villa at Bridgeport. The principal stress in his paper was upon the indefinite quality of the Gothic style which, unlike the Greek, did not set out to house the Deity in a material sense but, instead, attempted to make the unseen but omnipresent God of Christianity comprehensible to the inner man solely by implication. This is done through "loftiness of structure, the termination of which in every direction is . . . comparatively removed from the eye, [through] the tendency of the structure . . . continually upwards, without any well defined, but rather a suggested conclusion, leading the mind to the infinite above, which conveys the idea of God, not only beyond the limits of the building but beyond the limits of space appreciable to the physical sense." Eidlitz stated that the rectilinear ground plan of the classical temple lacks any point of religious focus. "Limited in all its boundaries" it "offers no particular place which may command the attention of the worshippers, and lead their minds to the one idea which forms the groundwork of their religious faith." He remarked that it was to remedy this defect, "and also to avoid a rectilinear termination of the building, which is artistically objectionable as too defined," that Christianity in its Gothic style substitutes a round or even better a polygonal termination of the east end, "which, by its artificial perspective, is more conducive to an apparently unlimited continuation of the building, while it presents an appropriately distinguished place for the performance of those ceremonies which constitute the most important part of Christian worship." [22]

For Eidlitz, as for Downing and Hopkins, the principal appeal of the

Gothic as an ecclesiastical style lay in its sublimity and limitlessness. Because of its lack of clearly defined boundaries it seemed to provide the most appropriate form for the church of an immaterial God. The style was favored by romanticists because it seemed congenial to their religious as well as their esthetic attitudes. Gothic architecture was better adapted to the romantic quest for infinite goals, for the not quite attainable, than classical styles, too constricted within sober, rational forms by clearly defined boundaries.

The changing attitude towards religion brought attacks upon the basic plan, as well as the styles, customarily used in Protestant churches. The traditional meeting-house conception was condemned in an article in the *Yale Literary Magazine*, which described the usual American church as "nothing more than a comfortable two story building, with a platform at one end for the speaker, and seats cushioned off for the choir, and a lecture-room underneath. In general," the article continued, "it presents a ludicrous mixture of church, theatre, and concert room, with a decided predominance in favor of the latter; and in truth it is well that it should be so, for it is used indiscriminately for every purpose under the sun." [23]

Probably the most radical assault upon the conventional American church plan was made by the New York Ecclesiological Society, an organization of high-church Episcopalians, and by those who shared its point of view. This organization was an offshoot of such English groups as the Cambridge Camden Society, later renamed the Ecclesiological Society, and the Oxford Architectural Society which advised, or, more accurately, dictated to, architects and clergymen about the arrangements necessary in Gothic churches to conform to the demands of high church ritual and of proper Christian symbolism.[24] Friedrich Schlegel had written of the connection between the Gothic style and Christian symbolism early in the century,[25] but the ecclesiologists codified Schlegel's insight into a set of rules which they imposed far and wide.

The attitude of the ecclesiologists toward Gothic architecture is exemplified by an article which appeared in *Putnam's Monthly* in 1853 describing the Medieval cathedrals as pervaded by Christian symbolism down to the chiselling of every separate stone and statue. "The cross formed the model for the ground plan. The idea of the Atonement was the animating heart of the whole, for necessarily dependent upon this is the other idea of the Trinity, which, with vitally organic power, concurred in vivifying the stony mass. Hence in so many of the old minsters, a nave and two side aisles: hence the body of the church and the transept: hence the triple windows in the east, each one containing a triple division: hence the three steps to the altar: hence the threefold division horizontally and vertically, of the façade. Everything," the article concluded, "was significant and symbolized, from the octagonal font of baptism near the entrance to the distorted figures sculptured upon the eaves and water-spouts." [26]

The program of the New York ecclesiologists, as announced in the first issue of their magazine, was to urge the adoption of the Gothic style of the fourteenth century, which they regarded as unequalled "for transparency of Christian truth and temper," and to disparage the use of other architectural styles "whether Grecian, Pagan or Romanesque." The ecclesiologists stressed the need of a clear separation of the church into two sections, the nave and the chancel, and a "proper development and proportionate expansion of each." [27] And although the nave was admitted to be a necessary part of the church for congregational worship, it was clearly considered of less importance than the chancel. Henry-Russell Hitchcock has explained how the desire for symbolic expression of the different religious functions by separation of various interior spaces, such as the nave and chancel, coincided with the picturesque taste for the complex exterior massing. A more articulated organization of interior space provided additional irregularity and variety for the exterior mass.[28]

Richard Upjohn, whose Trinity Church in New York established the Gothic as the customary style of the Episcopal church, was considerably influenced by ecclesiological principles. He belonged to the high church party and once, in 1846, refused to design a church for a Unitarian congregation in Boston on the grounds that their religious beliefs were too different from his.[29] Upjohn did his best to make his designs conform to the ritualistic ideas of the ecclesiologists and this sometimes caused trouble with low-church clients who preferred something closer to the old meeting-house type of church. Manton Eastburn, the rector of the Church of the Ascension in New York, bought the land adjoining the church property to the rear of the projected church building in order to forestall any attempt to give the structure a deep chancel of the sort Upjohn had designed for Trinity Church.[30]

On April 12, 1850, when involved with the designs for St. James Church, New London, Connecticut, Upjohn received two letters from Robert A. Hallam, the rector, protesting that he neither knew nor cared what Medieval usage recommended, but that he did know what was required by "propriety and common sense." He objected to the lectern which Upjohn intended to install and wrote that he had no intention to hold a book in his hand, that what he wanted was "a good serviceable Reading Desk, big enough to answer the purpose for which it is intended." In conclusion, he demanded that the two desks for the church be taken off the chancel floor and one of them be placed "in front of the Chancel pointing west, not less than six feet in width, three feet six inches high from the floor on which the minister stands, with a board in front wide enough to hold a folio Bible of the largest sort, and a folio Prayer Book." [31] A desk so placed would, of course, detract from the importance of the altar and emphasize the preaching rather than the ritualistic aspect of the church.

Despite the articulateness of the ecclesiologists their effect upon architecture in the United States was limited. Few architects followed their recommendations faithfully as did Upjohn, and in most Gothic churches, even those built for Roman and Anglo-Catholics, Medieval ground plans were adapted to modern congregational needs. The position of those favoring the free adaption of the Gothic style for modern churches was stated by an architect writing in the *Literary World* who objected to Anglicans claiming the Gothic as their private style and who wished it would be universally used. As a model for future Protestant Gothic churches, he praised St. George's Church, Stuyvesant Square, New York, which disregarded "orientation, depth of Chancel, triple division of Nave and Aisles, Pews and Galleries, all the Cambridge Camden requirements." "Here," he wrote, "we find no deep Chancel, because it is not intended to be filled either by a host of priests, or the whole body of communicants, no Altar Screen, because there is no Tabernacle of the holiest to be protected and displayed; no niches where there are no statues; no rood loft, because the Crucified is not here to be lifted except to the mental eye. Preaching, singing, and communing together, the requirements of modern worship are here represented and none other." [32]

Of considerable interest are the ecclesiastical manifestations of the organic theories of architecture which were fostered by the romantic reverence for nature. Despite the origin of functionalism in the scarcely orthodox religion of nature, it had, perhaps, an even greater influence upon Christian church buildings than upon ordinary secular architecture. The organic conceptions of architectural structure generally pervasive in the middle of the nineteenth century made any sort of dishonesty in construction of buildings intended for the worship of God seem not merely wrong but "criminal" and "wicked." [33] As early as 1841 both Pugin and the Cambridge Camden Society were insisting upon truth in church construction. Pugin wrote that although cast-iron, plaster, and composition ornaments painted to resemble oak or stone may be tolerable enough in a tea garden they "are utterly unworthy of a sacred edifice." He argued that no building erected to God should be made to appear superior through artificial means. "These are showy worldly expedients. . . . Nothing can be more execrable than making a church appear rich and beautiful in the eyes of man, but full of trick and falsehood, which cannot escape the all-searching eye of God, to whom churches should be built, and not to man." [34]

In 1848 Frank Willis, an architect born and trained in England, addressed the first meeting of the New York Ecclesiological Society on the subject "Reality in Architecture." Willis proposed that the society make *"Reality"* its watchword and fight "against all sham and miserable pharisaic pretensions." Exemplifying the way in which respect for materials and construction became a moral issue in the mid-nineteenth century, and the way in which esthetic matters were then identified with ethical ones, he declared that the society should determine to allow "no deception of any kind in a Church; deception being not only thoroughly unworthy so holy a structure, and repugnant to our ideas of reverence and propriety in anything consecrated to the Great God, but it is generally opposed to true taste." He spoke of buttresses added merely for show as "utterly despicable" and warned that simulated corner quoins should be avoided in timber churches because they are entirely incompatible with that material.[35]

The belief that church construction should be moral was not limited to Roman Catholics and high church Episcopalians, particularly after the publication of Ruskin's *The Seven Lamps of Architecture* in 1849. *A Book of Plans for Churches and Parsonages*, a book issued by the Congregational Churches in the United States in general convention, with designs by Upjohn, Downing, Renwick, Wheeler, and others, shows the influence of Ruskin and the other advocates of honesty in architecture. The Congregationalists, like the ecclesiologists, stressed the especial importance of truthfulness in church architecture. Of building materials they wrote, "if stone is not to be had for the walls of a house of worship, and bricks must be used, then let them be used openly and honestly, and not as though we are ashamed of them. So if only wood can be procured, or if its use is deemed expedient, let us not undertake, by bevelings, or painting and block-marks, to make it appear as if it were stone." They denied that wood is made more beautiful by paint or graining and stated that a number of common, native woods are esthetically pleasing in themselves and require "only trifling care in their selection, and a measure of good taste in their combination," to show the superiority of truthful treatment to expensive imitation.[36]

Protestant churches had in the United States borne the stamp of the meeting-house tradition until the effects of romanticism were fully felt. Before the middle of the nineteenth century, whether designed in the classical or quasi-Gothic styles, they had been marked by an asceticism typified by Asher Benjamin's belief that for them only "large bold, angular outlines" in dull colors were appropriate. But with the growing dissatisfaction with sober, rational religion, the traditional type of church lost favor. Whether or not the churches retained the preaching hall plan, there was a general recognition of the fact that a mere house for meeting was no longer suitable for Protestant worship. American Protestants accepted the dictum of the Catholic, Pugin, that religious structures should be *"more vast and beautiful than those in which they dwell."* [37] From that time on the senses were accepted into Protestant religious architecture; "form, color and sound [were to be permitted to] . . . contribute . . . toward the worship of God who made them all."

The admission of the senses into the Protestant church, which resulted from the nineteenth-century emphasis upon emotion rather than theology in religion, broadened the potentialities of American ecclesiastical architecture. The fact that the general level of quality of church architecture may actually have declined in the middle years of the century was due in the main to other aspects of romantic thought. The desire to create a dematerialized architecture as the most fitting for the worship of the unseen God of Christianity had, at other times, resulted in magnificent works of art such as the great Justinianic churches of Constantinople and Ravenna, the later Byzantine structures of eleventh century Greece, and the Medieval Gothic Cathedrals. But this same desire was dangerous in a period when formal coherence in architecture was already weakened by picturesque principles of design and by the associational sensibility. The picturesque emphasis on surfaces for their own sake severely reduced the value of surfaces as moulders of space and form. And a disregard of formal design resulted from the shift of emphasis from architectural forms to the romantic associations aroused by the forms.

In this connection, it is interesting to examine the churches of Richard Upjohn. His best exteriors do not suffer too much if compared with Medieval Gothic buildings, nor do certain of his interiors such as that of Trinity Church in New York, which is a reasonably faithful imitation of a Medieval interior although on a reduced scale and with a plaster vault. But the more original type of interior with open timber trusses which he customarily used in his maturity is a good deal less pleasing esthetically despite its structural honesty. The interior of St. Paul's Church of Buffalo which was built in 1850–51 is a good example of his work. The wooden

Trinity Church, New York, nave. (Photograph, Wurtz Brothers)

Winchester Cathedral, nave. (Photograph, Martin Hurlimann)

St. Paul's Church, Buffalo. Drawing by Richard Upjohn.
(Courtesy of Professor Everard M. Upjohn)

St. Paul's Church, Buffalo, interior.
(Photograph, courtesy of Professor Everard M. Upjohn)

structural elements are fussy, ugly, and formally incoherent, without a satisfactory esthetic relationship to the walls which are negated as plain solid forms by ornamentation. The interior exemplifies the havoc wrought upon ecclesiastical architecture by the desire for immateriality at a time when associationalism and the picturesque point of view dominated contemporary taste.

It is important to realize that, although many of the Gothic churches of the nineteenth century exemplify all too well the disintegration of form that accompanied the break up of post-Renaissance architectural traditions, they also have qualities which were to enter the new architectural synthesis. The stress on honesty of construction and the feeling for immateriality character-istic of Gothic revival churches were, with some modifications, to become a part of the program of the modern movement in architecture.

Notes

1. *The Works of John Adams,* II (Boston, 1850), 395.
2. Carleton Mabie, *The American Leonardo* (New York: Alfred A. Knopf, 1943), 131.
3. John Coolidge lists thirty-one Gothic churches constructed, chiefly in New York and New England between 1809 and 1839—Appendix A of his unpublished Harvard honors thesis "Gothic Revival Churches" (1935).
4. In 1805 Latrobe wrote that he proposed a Gothic design for a Catholic cathedral be-cause of "the veneration which the Gothic cathedrals generally excite by their peculiar style, by the associations belonging particularly to that style, and by the real grandeur and beauty which it possesses—Fiske Kimball, "Latrobe's Designs for the Cathedral of Baltimore," *Architectural Record,* vol. XLII, no. 6 (1917), 542. Among those who, in the twenties, wrote favorably of the Gothic style for Protestant churches were William Tudor (*Letters on the Eastern States* [New York, 1820], 157) and J. Fenimore Cooper (*Notions of the Americans,* 132).
5. *The Practical House Carpenter,* 95–96.
6. Signed "Observer," vol. IV, no. 6, 220.
7. Samuel G. Jarvis, *An Address, Delivered in the City of New Haven, at the Laying of the Cornerstone of Trinity Church, May 17, 1814* (New Haven, 1814); see also Town's own description of the church printed in John Henry Hobart's *The Moral Efficacy and the Positive Benefits* (New Haven, 1816), 25–29.
8. *Things as They Are* (New York, 1834), 246.
9. *Essay on Gothic Architecture,* 1–2.
10. *The Diary of Philip Hone,* II, 754; cited by Wayne Andrews, *Architecture, Ambi-tion and Americans* (New York: Harper & Brothers, 1955), 130.
11. In a speech at the laying of the cornerstone of the Mount Vernon Church printed in part in the *Boston Daily Advertiser,* November 24, 1843 (no. 125), 2. I was directed to this speech and to the architectural controversy following it by Professor Oscar Handlin.
12. *A Step from the New World to the Old* (New York, 1852), I, 173; II, 56–58.
13. "Architects and Architecture," vol. XLIX, no. 161 (September, 1850), 285–286. See also M. Field, *City Architecture* (New York, 1853); Horace Greeley, *Glances at Europe*

(New York, 1851), 78; H. Mattison, "Methodist Church Architecture," *The National Magazine*, vol. VII (Dec., 1855), 499.

14. Pugin wrote, "not only are the details of modern churches borrowed from Pagan instead of Christian antiquity, but the very plan and arrangement of the buildings themselves are now fashioned after a heathen temple; for which unsightly and inappropriate form modern churchmen and architects have abandoned those which are not only illustrative of the great mysteries of the Christian faith, but whose use has been sanctioned by the custom of more than twelve centuries." He continued, "these temples were erected for an idolatrous worship, and were suited only for the idolatrous rites which were performed in them. The interior entered only by the priests, was comparatively small, and either dark or open at the top, while the peristyle and porticoes were spacious, for the people who assisted without. There is not the slightest similarity between our worship and the idolatrous worship of the Greeks. We require that the people should be *within* the church, not outside. If, therefore, you adopt a perfect Greek temple, your interior will be confined and ill-suited for the intended purpose, while your exterior will occasion an enormous outlay without any utility. If, on the other hand, you strip a Greek temple of its external peristyle, and build your external walls in the place of the pillars, you entirely destroy the most beautiful feature of the architecture, and the building becomes a miserable departure from the style it professes to imitate. . . . The Greeks did not introduce windows in their temples; they are essentially necessary to us. Perforate the walls with windows, and you again destroy the simplicity and unity of Greek architecture, which its admirers extol as one of its greatest beauties—*The True Principles of Pointed or Christian Architecture*, 46–47. An article in the *New York Review* in 1841, the year Pugin's book was published, quoted Pugin at length and concluded that the propriety of the Greek style for Christian churches "is at least questionable"—"Rural Church Edifices," vol. IX, no. 17, 184–185.

15. *Boston Daily Advertiser*, November 17, 1843 (no. 119), 1. Unsigned but close enough to the position Gilman expressed in "Architecture in the United States" to be recognized as his. An article published eleven days later which was signed A.D.G. refers to a "former article" published in the paper a few days before.

16. *Boston Daily Advertiser*, November 24, 1843 (no. 125), 2.

17. "Unity of Architecture," a paper read to the American Institute of Architects, printed in *The Crayon*, vol. VI, no. 3 (1859), 86–87.

18. *A Paper on New England Architecture* (Boston, 1858), 24.

19. Issue of November 24, 1843 (no. 125), 2. See also "Ecclesiastical Architecture," *Yale Literary Magazine*, vol. XI, no. 2 (1845), 69.

20. *The Old World and the New* (New York, 1836), 81–84.

21. "A Short Chapter on Country Churches," *Rural Essays*, 262–263.

22. "Christian Architecture" published in *The Crayon*, vol. V, no. 2 (1858), 53–54.

23. "Ecclesiastical Architecture," *loc. cit.*, 70–71.

24. Cf. Clark, *The Gothic Revival*, ch. VIII, especially 200–221. Designs for at least two churches in the United States, St. Mark's in Philadelphia and St. James the Less in Falls of Schuylkill, Pennsylvania, were sent from England by the Cambridge Camden Society. —Cf. Coolidge, *op. cit.*, 149, 169.

25. Schlegel wrote that the Christian architecture of the Middle Ages expresses "the elevation of holy thoughts, the loftiness of meditation set free from earth and proceeding unfettered to the heavens. . . . But this is not all; every part of the structure is as symbolical as the whole. . . . The altar is directed towards the rising sun, and the three great entrances are meant to express the conflux of worshippers from all the regions of the earth. Three towers express the Christian mystery of the triune Godhead. The choir rises like a temple within a temple of redoubled loftiness. The shape of the cross is in common with Christian churches of even earlier times. . . . The rose is the essential part of all the ornament of this architecture. . . . When we view the whole structure, from the crypt to the choir, it is impossible to resist the idea of earthly death leading only to the fulness, the freedom, the solemn glories of eternity"—*Lectures on the History of Literature*, 337–339.

26. "On the Gothic Style in the Fine Arts," vol. II, no. 8, 192. See also J. Coleman Hart,

Designs for Parish Churches (New York, 1857), 18–19, 21. The founders of the Cambridge Camden Society, J. M. Neale and Benjamin Webb, translated the Medieval treatise by Durandus, *The Symbolism of Churches and Church Ornaments* (Leeds, 1843). Neale and Webb's lengthy introductory essay discusses many aspects of church symbolism.

27. "Cheap Churches," *The New York Ecclesiologist,* vol. I, no. 1, 5–6.

28. *Early Victorian Architecture in Britain,* 101, 155.

29. The Federal Street, later the Arlington Street Church, of Boston of which Ezra Stiles Gannett succeeded William Ellery Channing as minister in 1842. Everard M. Upjohn, *Richard Upjohn, Architect and Churchman* (New York: Columbia University Press, 1939), 81–87.

30. *Ibid.,* 69. Eastburn later became rector of Trinity Church, Boston and Bishop of Massachusetts.

31. *Ibid.,* 77–79.

32. The architect-author was possibly Cary Long. "Architectonics," vol. III, nos. 94 and 95 (1848), 833, 853–854. See also Henry M. Dexter, *Meeting Houses Considered Historically and Suggestively* (Boston, 1859), 20.

33. "Architecture," *The Crayon,* vol. III, no. 5 (1856), 150.

34. *Op. cit.,* 45, 46.

35. *New York Ecclesiologist,* vol. I, no. 1, 10, 12.

36. *A Book of Plans for Churches and Parsonages* (New York, 1853), 21–22.

37. *Op. cit.,* 44.

5
Nationalism and a
New Architecture

IN 1840 ALEXIS DE TOCQUEVILLE WROTE THAT DEMOCRATIC NATIONS, WHICH
have little superfluous wealth and have a universal desire for comfort, "will
habitually prefer the useful to the beautiful, and . . . will require that the
beautiful be useful." [1] Suggestive of modern American functionalism as de
Tocqueville's generalization is, it bore slight relation to the mass of revivalist
architecture he had seen on his visit to the United States. Gothic revival
theory may have anticipated recent functionalist theories, but it is hard to
see any strong predominance of the useful over the beautiful in actual Romantic buildings, whether castellated country houses or temple-porticoed
public edifices. Not until about the middle of the century, under the pressure
of the needs of expanding commercial and industrial activity, were any important structural innovations made in the United States. And even then the
skeletally supported cast iron buildings were clothed with conventionally
"beautiful" Renaissance ornament.

Ultimately an architecture unlike any of the past took shape in the United
States as a result of the conjunction of functionalist theories and the new
building materials which were used with increasing frequency. Important
in the development of the new American architecture was national and tem-
poral patriotism, the belief that only a revolutionary type of design could

give satisfactory expression to the civilization of nineteenth-century America. For decades, however, nationalism made slight impression upon architecture. It was the last of the beliefs of romanticism to make itself felt in an important way.

Despite the ceaseless American concern with national character, defined almost exclusively in opposition to Europe, nationalistic sentiments are almost entirely lacking in early American architectural writings. There were no demands for a new architectural language different from that of Europe; no Noah Webster called for America to become as independent architecturally as she was politically. There was no architectural monument analogous to Joel Barlow's Americanist epic, *The Vision of Columbus*. American architects in the years after the Revolution followed European styles instead of trying to invent anything adapted to the national aspirations of the young country. Amateurs of architecture like Thomas Jefferson and Nicholas Biddle pushed to its most extreme form the latest international style, the classical revival.

But occasionally attempts were made to modify the traditional orders of classical architecture and to create an order more appropriate for the United States. The earliest "American order" was that designed by a Frenchman, Major L'Enfant, for Federal Hall, the former New York City hall which was rebuilt in 1789 as the original national capitol. Better known than L'Enfant's introduction of the symbols of the American republic into the classical orders is Latrobe's use of American vegetation in designing original quasi-Corinthian capitals in his reconstruction of the capitol after its destruction by the British in 1814.[2] These capitals which were placed in the old Senate entrance and rotunda had their bells decorated with corn cobs and tobacco leaves, respectively, at the suggestion of ex-President Jefferson.

Such attempts to Americanize classical forms were few in number and without appreciable effect upon architectural developments. Jefferson, who exerted the most important single influence upon the course of architecture in the United States in the early years of the Republic, was no cultural nationalist. Characteristic was his writing to Madison that he had selected the Maison Carrée as model for his Richmond capitol because it had "obtained the approbation of fifteen or sixteen centuries, and is therefore preferable to any design which might be newly contrived."[3]

Americans might from time to time associate the architecture of many periods of European history, beginning with the Roman of the Empire, with despotism and corruption in government, but they never rejected European architecture in totality as unsuitable for American use. The classical styles gained support from their association with the ancient republics. And, entirely apart from this association, the unadorned Greek style, especially, seemed appropriate for a country with a simple republican form of government. It seemed natural enough, therefore, to regard the Greek revival, the latest European architectural movement, as peculiarly suited to become the American national style.

But the climate and conditions prevalent in the Greek republics differed considerably from those of the United States. The architecture of classical temples was only occasionally suitable, without drastic modifications, for the purposes of nineteenth-century America. And in the years after 1840 attacks upon the Greek revival began to multiply. The inconveniences inherent in reconciling the temple form to the modern need of windows and chimneys had been tolerated during the dominance of the post-Lockean taste for clearly defined classical forms, but they seemed beyond endurance once the picturesque esthetic had become supreme.[4] The extent to which the Greek style had passed out of favor by the middle fifties is indicated by a description in *Putnam's Monthly* of classical banks on Wall Street as "tough, granite dowagers," remnants of the *"ancien régime"* with "bulky and ungraceful leg-like columns, out of place, out of proportion, like a crowd of briefly-petticoated ballet dancers, who stand shivering and unregarded after the play and its applauses are over, for their carriages to carry them home." [5]

With the growing dissatisfaction with classical architecture, there began a demand for a new architecture more suited to the national character and needs. Nationalism, a potent force in American literature between the time of Noah Webster and Whitman's first preface to *Leaves of Grass*, was not really felt in architecture during the period in which the classical revival styles were considered particularly appropriate for public buildings. But once the revival fell before the picturesque revolution in taste and the scathing criticism of writers such as Arthur Gilman, nationalism became as important in architectural as in literary theory.

It is reflected in the writings of romantic naturalists. In 1841 Emerson asked "Why need we copy the Doric or the Gothic model? Beauty, convenience, grandeur of thought and quaint expression are as near to us as to any." He spoke with the conviction that a satisfactory national architecture was within reach if only the American artist would set to work freshly, following hints provided by "the climate, the soil, the length of the day, the wants of the people, [and] the habit and form of government." [6]

Nationalism is also notable in writings not especially influenced by natural-
ism. It is strongly present in the most significant architectural manifesto of
1841, Robert Cary Long's article, "On the Alleged Degeneracy of Modern
Architecture," which appeared in the *Journal of the Franklin Institute*.[7]
What is meant by the degeneracy of modern architecture, Long asked. "Is it
degenerate because it is not Greek, not Palladian, not Elizabethan, not
Egyptian?" Would the architecture of Greece have become what it did if
Greek architects "had not given free room for the genius of their country,
and its institutions, to manifest itself architecturally?" We have now in
America, Long declared, specimens of every style that ever existed. "But
has this endless repetition of the architecture of the past, any title to be called
the architecture of the present? . . . Architecture must manifest the changes
that are taking place in society, the greater ones, we hope and believe, that
are to come. . . . Architecture must grow naturally, its own peculiar tenden-
cies must be observed, and it must be trained accordingly. . . . Let us all try
to see which of us will first produce something in the art peculiar—characteristic—suited to the age—national." [8]

It was, however, one thing to assert the need of a national architecture and
another to break through the fetters of nineteenth-century eclecticism to
achieve an original style. Many years were to pass after 1841 before anything
resembling a distinctive American school of architecture was to come into
being. The associational values which still exerted a powerful influence upon
American taste in the middle decades of the century were difficult to over-
come. Typical of the esthetic confusion of the period was a letter to *The
Crayon* in which the writer states that "failure is inherent in the very nature
of imitative art" but urged the exact imitation of village churches of France
and England for American use declaring that he longed "to see in this young
country some repetitions of the model churches of the old world." [9]

In mid-nineteenth century America, most architects believed that any
new architecture would have to grow gradually from the traditional styles.
Downing attacked those "who put on a hypocritical air, and sit in judgement
on the progress . . . of the building taste in this country" decrying everything foreign and demanding something entirely new "as if an architecture
sprang up like the after-growth in our forests, the natural and immediate
consequence of clearing the soil."

Downing wrote that all the known styles of architecture are

local modifications of the styles of the older countries, from which the newer colony
borrowed them, as the climate, habits of the people, and genius of the architects, *acting
upon each other through a long series of years,* gradually developed into such styles. It is,

therefore, as absurd for the critics to ask for the *American style of architecture,* as it was for the English friends of a Yankee of our acquaintance to request him . . . to do them the favor to put on his savage dress and talk a little American! This country is, indeed, too distinct in its institutions, and too vast in its territorial and social destinies, not to shape out for itself a great national type in character, manners and art; but the development of the finer and more intellectual traits are slower in a nation than they are in a man, and only time can develop them healthily in either case.

We are at present, he continued, in "what may be called the experimental stage of architectural taste. With the passion for novelty, and the feeling of independence that belong to this country, our people seem determined *to try everything.*" [10]

Gervase Wheeler, like Downing, believed in the gradual evolution of an American style from the picturesque rural styles of Europe. And he thought that American buildings were already noticeably different from their European prototypes. "The materials and other requirements here wreath themselves into modified forms . . . [for example] where honestly developed, the modern Italian style of American Villas comes in different aspect from the architect's hand than [it would in Europe.]" [11]

Although the belief that the national style would develop from the rural cottage and villa styles was common during the prevalence of the picturesque esthetic, other styles were also favored as models. The Renaissance palazzo style, most popular urban style of the forties and fifties, was backed by Arthur Gilman who preferred the Gothic for churches. Renaissance architecture seemed to Gilman readily adaptable for nineteenth-century secular uses. It was a modern style able, unlike ancient classical architecture, to achieve notable esthetic results without inconvenient and expensive columns and porticoes.[12] On the other hand Robert Dale Owen argued that only in Medieval architecture could be found the flexibility necessary to any style which was to be suitable as a national style.[13]

The arguments of the proponents of Gothic architecture are of particular interest in view of the relationship between the theories of structure of the Gothic revival and the functional ideas later so important in American architecture. Anticipatory of the developed functionalism of Louis Sullivan and showing the influence of the structural rationalism of the great French Gothicist, Viollet-le-Duc, was the position of Leopold Eidlitz. In a discussion held by the American Institute of Architects concerning the style for a proposed New York City Hall, he defended Gothic construction against Detlef Lienau, a classicist who had been trained by Henri Lâbrouste and who is noted as an innovator in using French Second Empire style. Eidlitz argued that if improvements upon Gothic construction are possible they are to be sought only "in the exertion of architects taking that style as a basis of operations." He then suggested that it was probably mere quibbling over terms that led some of the members of the Institute to oppose the Gothic style and proposed that they substitute for the term Gothic the definition, "that style of architecture which teaches construction adapted to purpose and organization, with ornamentation to express the construction." [14]

Close as Eidlitz seems to the central theories of later architects like Sullivan, there was no real chance of the Gothic revival forming the basis for the national American architecture of the future. It had no connection with the national past. The Gothic could seem a French style to the French, an English style to the English, a German style to the Germans, but it could never really seem an American style to Americans. Gothic structures dominated ecclesiastical architecture in the United States but they never were as widely used for secular purposes as in England. The real importance of the Gothic revival for future architectural developments in the United States lay in the functionalist theories propounded by its supporters, which were to have a profound effect upon the young Frank Lloyd Wright.[15]

The nationalistic sentiments which the Gothic revival could not call on for support did begin to appear in architectural writings of the fifties. The turning to the colonial past for a national architectural tradition became important only about the time of the centennial of 1876, and the full blight of the colonial revival was not felt until the late eighties, but certain signs of the impending cult of architectural ancestor worship appeared at mid-century. One of the most interesting of the early cultural nationalists was a writer for *Putnam's Monthly*. Believing like Herder that great art comes spontaneously from the people, he traced the great architecture of all countries "to its original type, in the farm house or the barn" and asserted that "we shall find the same fact awaiting us in America, where the only really good houses are the old farm houses of the Dutch and English type . . . testifying to the worth of simplicity, and the beauty of common sense in the midst of pretense and gingerbread work." Little dreaming of the future success of the colonial revival, he continued, "we fear there is as little chance of a return to the solidity and largeness of our grandfather's architecture as there is of a revival of the sincerity and simplicity of their lives." [16]

Of more ultimate significance in the history of architectural theory than the anticipators of the nostalgically nationalistic revivalism of the twentieth century were those who believed that an architecture worthy of the United

States would be achieved only through creating structures adapted to contemporary needs in the same way as natural things are adapted to the multifold purposes of nature. The most interesting of these naturalistic theorists of architecture, Horatio Greenough, was no admirer of "the old, bald, neutraltoned, Yankee farm house" [17] and was even less happy about the revivalistic architecture of his time. He wrote that the mind of America, engaged in more pressing matters, has never been properly applied to architectural design.[18] Like Emerson and Cooper he was as delighted by the products of American craftsmanship [19] as he was upset by the state of American architecture. Greenough was dismayed that a nation that has "reduced locomotion to its simplest elements, in the trotting wagon and the yacht *America*" should be content to receive its notions of architecture, as it does its fashions of dress and forms of entertainment, from Europe.[20] He attributed the American superiority in practical design to the necessity there of adapting the form to natural forces. "In all structure that from its nature is purely scientific, in fortifications, in bridges, in shipbuilding, we have been emancipated from authority by the stern organic requirements of the works. The modern wants spurned the traditional formula in these structures, as the modern life outgrew the literary moulds of Athens." [21] If Americans would bring to their architecture the seriousness that shapes their shipbuilding, they would soon have structures as superior to the Parthenon, for modern purposes, as the frigate *Constitution* is to the ship of the Argonauts.[22] Greenough denied "that the style pointed out by our mechanics is what is sometimes miscalled an economical, a cheap style." It is rather, he wrote, "the dearest of all styles. It costs the thought of men, much, very much thought, untiring investigation, ceaseless experiment." [23] He believed that the work, thought, and experiment involved were necessary if contemporary architectural problems were to be solved. No longer should the United States import its architectural solutions from Europe, ready made. An architecture appropriate for Americans will be created only when the "redundant . . . [is] pared down, the superfluous dropped, the necessary itself reduced to its simplest expression," and we then find, whatever the organization may be, the essential beauty that waited for us until we had accomplished our task.[24]

Actual building in the middle years of the century fell well short of the vision of Horatio Greenough, but it gradually broke from the fetters of archeological imitation and some progress was made toward a functionally oriented American architecture unshaped by traditional European prototypes. Although the picturesque rural architecture sponsored by Downing and the

House at Mount Desert, Maine, by William Ralph Emerson;
engraving, American Architect, 5, 1879.

Summer House, Bar Harbor, Maine, by William Ralph Emerson.
Engraving, Builder, Dec. 25, 1886.

Project for a "House by the Sea" by John Calvin Stevens. Engraving, Stevens and Cobb,
Examples of American Domestic Architecture.

other writers of house plan books was nourished by an eclectic English architectural movement, it gradually grew away from dependence upon historical precedent and expressed its wooden frame construction in a free and non-derivative way. From the start, as Wheeler perceived, certain modifications were made in European designs to adapt them to the American climate and living conditions.

Perhaps the most notable characteristic of American, as opposed to English, rural houses was the wide use of porches. As early as 1842 Downing had stressed the indispensability of porches in the hot American summers,[25] and though rare in English designs, they were almost invariably present in American ones. Later, as rural architecture became more emancipated from close imitation of any of the traditional styles, porches became an integral part of the architectural expression of the house. In the late seventies and the eighties spatial innovation was not limited to the use of deeply shaded porches which swept out in various directions and served to bring masses of the enveloping air within the houses' irregular bulk. Plans became less tight and regular and were characterized by an increasingly free handling of the flow of interior space. Vincent Scully calls this architecture the "Shingle Style" because of the unpainted wooden shingles dramatically used to cover the sprawling, irregular masses, the huge roofs, rounded towers and angular gables.[26]

Roughly contemporary with the maturing of this picturesque housing was the emergence of the Chicago school of commercial architects, the first Americans to give architectural expression to the unique characteristics of metal construction. The Chicago school is more closely related to the modern movement than to romantic architecture, yet it has interesting antecedents in earlier nineteenth-century theory of metal design. The use of iron on a large scale, made possible by the industrial revolution, began in England and in France. Tom Paine devised a scheme for an arched bridge of considerable span with cast-iron panels acting as voussoirs and took it to England, at the advice of Benjamin Franklin, in the hope that it could be erected there where industrialism was further advanced than in the United States.[27] Jefferson mentioned Paine's bridge as one of the two greatest American inventions in the arts and declared that it "promises to be cheaper by a great deal than stone, and to admit of a much greater arch." [28]

In 1818 John Haviland predicted that the introduction of cast iron might well create a wholly new sort of architecture,[29] but when, a dozen or so years later, he designed the first cast-iron façade in the United States, for a bank in

Pottsville, Pennsylvania, he tried to make the iron work resemble stone. Haviland described the façade as having moulded cornices of cast iron which imitate marble and consisting in the main of iron plates which were "cast in lengths and form corresponding with the size and jointing of stone-work." He wrote that after it was finished "the whole was well painted and sanded with white sand, which gave the surface a very beautiful and uniform texture of stone, free from gloss, and at the same time prevented its rusting."

Although iron gained respect as a building material between the time when Haviland wrote in 1833 and the middle fifties, it was generally disguised to resemble the conventional building materials, perishable wood, or expensive marble or sandstone. Haviland had proclaimed that it was "not only more fire-proof, durable, and stronger, than wood, but also more economical and favorable to embellishment, than the marble or cut free-stone" because when duplicate ornaments are needed the work expended on one mould was all that was required.[30] Most architects followed the lead of Haviland and took full advantage of the ease with which traditional stone ornament could be reproduced in cast iron.

Representative of the general disregard for the properties of metal which endured until the middle of the century was the Penn Mutual Life Insurance Building in Philadelphia (1850–51). Here a cast-iron facade was erected with small windows and broad areas of wall, according to a design originally intended for execution in masonry. James Bogardus, the best known of American constructors of iron buildings, shared in the general ambivalence toward iron, combining traditionalism in ornament with radical innovation in structure. Bogardus's earliest cast-iron fronts seem partially adapted to their material. They were much more open than the Penn Mutual façade, consisting largely of rows of windows each separated from its neighbors by narrow piers faced with engaged columns. Between the strips of windows were fairly wide horizontal bands of metal. These bands contained ornamental panels beneath each window, and under the panels were appliquéd blind arches which met the engaged columns adorning the row of windows below. The Harper and Brothers Building (1854), the most famous of Bogardus's iron fronts, was largely derived from R. G. Hatfield's Sun Building in Baltimore (1851).[31] This influential structure of Hatfield's was rectangular with walls almost entirely of glass, yet its general effect was most unlike the glass cages of recent years. The design was based loosely on Venetian palace façades. A bristling profusion of engaged columns, panels, arch mouldings and keystones, knobby pedestal and entablature blocks, statues and powerful

Harper and Brothers Building, New York. (Courtesy Harper and Row)

Sun Building, Baltimore. (Photograph, courtesy of Enoch Pratt Free Library)

consoles gave it an excessively agitated appearance. Something of this rest-lessness, which perhaps reflects a struggle of the picturesque taste against con-fining rectangularity, continued to characterize iron fronted and metal framed buildings well into the eighties.

For Bogardus and other mid-century builders in iron, one of the principal advantages of the material was the ease with which it reproduced the great profusion of ornament which delighted contemporary taste. John W. Thom-son, in a pamphlet written on Bogardus's behalf, stated that multiplication of similar decorations is even cheaper in iron than in wood and that, in addi-tion, the decorations "will retain their original fullness and sharpness of out-line long after those in stone have decayed or disappeared. Fluted columns and Corinthian capitals, the most elaborate carvings, and the richest designs, which the architect may have dreamed of, but did not dare represent in his plans, may thus be reproduced for little more than the cost of ordinary castings." [32]

Whatever may have been the effect of iron upon the design of bridges and other utilitarian structures, in formal architecture its introduction pro-duced no immediate transformation apart from a general thinning and lightening of framing members. In a period when the historic styles retained an associational allure and picturesque taste delighted in rich and intricate decorative effects, the use of iron in buildings which were designed to be of artistic value merely facilitated the manufacture of ornament derived from traditional Greek, Gothic or Renaissance sources. One influential architec-tural doctrine of the mid-nineteenth century, however, worked against the effect of associationism and the picturesque and helped produce a demand for the use of iron in new clean forms rather than the old cluttered ones. The belief that the intrinsic qualities of natural materials should be respected by the designers of buildings, which had its roots in the naturalism of Words-worth and Emerson, led to the conviction that the use of a radically different material called for a radically new architecture.

Despite his own practice, John Haviland, in a moment of vision as early as 1818, had seen that the use of iron would have a serious effect upon architectural developments.[33] But after Haviland, American architectural writers had little to say about iron until the middle of the century. In 1849 Robert Dale Owen remarked that the traditional building materials, wood, brick, and stone, each imparted a distinctive character to the buildings for which they were used, and suggested that the use of iron, a new material with unique properties of its own, might revolutionize architecture.[34]

A few years later James Freeman Clarke's admiration for the iron station house at Ghent and the iron bridge nearby moved him to similar insight. "While modern pedants are copying the medieval arches and buttresses," he wrote, "the spirit of our times may be creating unobserved a style of architecture hitherto unknown." Clarke thought that iron structures have "an airy lightness" which can never be achieved in stone and remarked that the reason spectators rebel at the new iron spire on Rouen Cathedral is because "it seems too light and open to be in harmony with the rest of the structure."

Clarke's remarks on iron architecture illustrate the way in which the Emersonian doctrine of respect for materials clashed with the picturesque love of lush ornamentation. After stating that the use of a new material, metal, may well produce a totally new style of building, he went on to stress the ease with which the naturalistic ornament that he admired could be multiplied in cast iron. "The whole front of a building may be wreathed with vines and foliage, while its roof is decorated with a thousand spires and pinnacles overhung with blossoms and fruit. In fact there need be no limit to this sort of decoration." [35]

In 1856 an article appearing in *The Crayon* marked a new development in American thinking about metal architecture. Previous writers had sensed in a vague way that an architecture of metal would be different from the traditional ones of stone. The writer of this article made a strong plea for the honest use of metal, understanding that the possibilities of a metal architecture could be realized only if the inherent qualities of the material were respected. The painting of iron columns to resemble stone in Duncan and Sherman's new bank in New York was attacked by him as an absurdity, as was the covering of a fireproof ceiling "with wood-furring . . . to produce an imitation of supporting beams where there are none." He continued, "What, ashamed of the very merits of the building! and thus attempt to hide the honest iron beams and girders, instead of decorating them truthfully and artistically! When will architects begin to think more and copy less?" [36]

The one building which did most to awaken the nineteenth century to the esthetic possibilities of a new architecture based upon the straightforward use of the new materials, iron and glass, was the great structure which Joseph Paxton had designed for the International Exhibition of 1851 at London. The Crystal Palace, which was imitated almost immediately for the New York World's Fair of 1853, seemed the perfect embodiment of the romantic

Crystal Palace, London. Etching.

Crystal Palace, New York. Lithograph, the J. Clarence Davies Collection,
Museum of the City of New York.

desire for immateriality in architecture.[37] The immaterial quality of the Gothic had seemed to many Americans to qualify it as the only style suitable for Christian worship. And many American visitors were attracted by this quality in Paxton's building and saw at once the revolution in architecture it presaged. Horace Greeley concerned himself more with the practical than the magical aspects of the "fairy wonder." He stated that not only is the structure "better adapted to its purpose than any other edifice ever yet built could be, but it combines remarkable cheapness with vast and varied utility. Depend on it, stone and timber will have to stand back for iron and glass hereafter, to an extent not yet conceivable. The triumph of Paxton is perfect, and heralds a revolution." [38]

The most appreciative American description of the Crystal Palace appeared in an article in *Putnam's Monthly*. The structure seemed, the writer stated, "rather like an exhalation of the dawn than a building made with hands. It looked not at first as of the earth, earthy—but as of the air, ethereal—only separated from it by the thinnest film of materiality—and yet—on a closer view, it was found substantial, vast and endurable. Buoyant as a bubble in its appearance, it needed only to be touched, to awaken the profoundest convictions of its reality and strength. Those firm iron pillars, and those compact and riveted joints, binding and supporting its immeasurable façades of glass, were the marriage of power with beauty, and more than any other structure that we ever saw, impressed us with a sense of man's infinite ingenuity." The building was, the critic declared, "the first original piece of architecture in modern times . . . new alike in its materials and in its mode and style of construction . . . though of a length greater than that of any building that had been before attempted, and covering a larger area than Karnac, the Pyramids, or St. Peter's—it was entirely novel, because perfectly adapted to its ends." [39]

Of greater significance than this amateur's wonderful excitement of discovery was a paper read to the American Institute of Architects in 1858. The reader, Henry Van Brunt, who later shared in the design of Harvard's Victorian Gothic Memorial Hall, displayed a professional's understanding of the implications of metal frame construction. His paper strikingly demonstrates how the romantic respect for metallic building materials, a respect based ultimately upon a reverence for all the things of nature, anticipated many of the principles of modern architecture. He began by declaring that in the best periods of architecture respect had always been paid to the "nature, attributes and capacities" of building materials. He stated that in the buildings of the thirteenth century there was a proper fusion of "nature's innate powers" and the adaptive skill of man, and that the decline of the Gothic style began when the carvers violated the intrinsic qualities of the stone and made it "smile and flutter under the chisel." Now, he wrote, with the rapid advance of the science of construction, the requirements of many modern buildings are such that they can be properly met only by recourse to constructive and architectural features which have no precedent in either the classical or the Medieval past. And a revolution in esthetic expression should accompany "each new mechanical or constructive means placed in our hands."

Hitherto, he wrote, architects have used iron only in trusses and secretively in concealed anchors and ties. To base a system of architecture upon honest use of the material has been out of the question. But this has been called " 'a cast iron age' " so why not create an architecture of cast iron to express it? Van Brunt argued that the repetitiousness inevitable in iron decoration, which has previously caused it to be condemned, is actually perfectly expressive of the modern age.

In anticipation of more recent worshippers of the machine, he stated that the present is a period of aggregates rather than one of individualities, that "it is not one of barbarous sacrifice either of time, labor, money or material [as Ruskin might have preferred], but of wise economy. Science has nearly destroyed personal labor, and has substituted the labor of machinery, and almost all the industrial arts are carried on not by hands but by machines. . . . Therefore the architecture, to express our spirit best, is not one of personal thought and aspiration in the workmen . . . but rather one of system, and, as regards the workman one of organized subordination; it is essentially an architecture of strict mechanical obedience." Such a mechanical architecture, Van Brunt wrote, would be "one of strict unities and formal repetitions, as expressive of the mechanical means by which it is produced." And these characteristics are particularly representative of a period which, unlike the Ancient or Medieval Periods, desires neither emotional impulse nor instruction from its buildings and requires "little more than the pure architectural expression of fitness for its peculiar purposes."

Van Brunt suggested that if the need arose to express the formal and stately in iron construction, a starting point for an honest architecture could be found in certain Gothic forms, for example in the panel work of the Florentine Duomo and campanile and of the English perpendicular cathedrals. But, he continued, let it not be forgotten, while using old models as guides for modern buildings, that many old rules of architecture must be modified if the constructive properties of iron are to be respected. The "exact laws of superimposition, intercolumniation, proportion by module, and the like, which have hitherto held tyrranical sway over all our composition" are based upon stone construction which limits the width of openings and requires that masses be piled perpendicularly upon each other with careful separation of weight among the arches and with the lighter elements upon the heavier. Those traditional principles of design do not, he wrote, hold true for iron construction which admits "masses over voids as well as voids over masses . . . downward thrusts of almost any force upon any point of its arches without fear of fracture, [and] almost any width of aperture . . . and almost any slenderness of supports." [40]

The new decorative system based upon nineteenth-century developments in constructive science which Van Brunt heralded took time in coming. His own designs conformed to the patterns of contemporary eclecticism. Earlier works, on which he collaborated with William R. Ware, included a handsome railroad station in Worcester and the Episcopal Theological Seminary in Cambridge in the Gothic style. Later his firm followed the Romanesque and Renaissance styles as they became popular, contributing the classicistic Electricity Building to the World's Columbian Exposition at Chicago. During Van Brunt's lifetime a new American architecture based upon the inherent qualities of metal did begin to develop as a group of Chicago architects met the problem of creating multi-storied buildings for modern business.

Despite its early success the architecture of Chicago did not quickly sweep away the less fortunate aspects of romantic architectural design. Instead the new movement had to struggle for its life against a resurgence of romantic eclecticism. The disillusionment with the present and nostalgia for the past common at the turn of the century, and so notable in writers like Mark Twain and Henry Adams, was reflected in enthusiasm for Medieval, Renaissance, and early American architecture. The "American Renaissance" and the colonial revival together dominated American building for decades and destroyed the career of as great an architect as Louis Sullivan. As late as 1927 a historian of American architecture could write of "Louis Sullivan and the Lost Cause." [41] And the force of romantic associationism has continued to shape the bulk of American design down to the present moment.

A review of romantic architectural thought, looking back from mid-century theories of metal construction to the classical revivalism of Jefferson, which was both radical and cosmopolitan, discloses immense diversity and considerable uncertainty. The buildings of the intervening period, frequently attractive and even compelling, but often disconcerting, face both the past and the future. All the arts are forever in flux, developing and changing, never adhering for long to any fixed set of principles, but the architecture shaped by the romantic sensibility is notably transitional. The earlier nineteenth century saw the abandonment of traditions of design which had descended from the Renaissance and the beginnings of new conceptions which led directly to the modern movement which was inaugurated in the 1880's.

The varied intellectual currents of Romanticism destroyed the old architecture and prepared the way for the new. In a period when most people based their esthetic judgments upon chance associations aroused by works of art, the concern for formal relations characteristic of both the baroque and academic strains of post-Renaissance architecture gave way. Under the influence of the associationist habit of mind and the awakened interest in history, the classicism of the Enlightenment was transformed. Too often romantic classicism became a matter of copying elements from specific classical buildings and of stimulating sentimental reveries about the past instead of designing buildings according to generally valid principles derived from the ancients. The literal imitation of ancient forms, entirely apart from its repressive effect upon creative design, brought almost insurmountable architectural problems. Only occasionally could modern needs be accommodated gracefully within structures of a classical type. Compromises had to be made, and frequently the very features which gave classical buildings their distinction were sacrificed without achieving anything which satisfactorily met modern functional requirements.

The picturesque esthetic which originated in the romantic reverence for natural scenery was another contributor to the destruction of the principles of form which had traditionally governed western architecture. Picturesque architects attempted to diminish the geometrical quality of their buildings so that they would merge more easily with natural settings. For the same reason these architects were possessed with a *horror vacui*, believing that the formal emphases customary in post-Renaissance architecture would contrast too sharply with the natural environment. Whatever sense the picturesque deformalization of architecture made in country dwellings, it had little justification in monumental city buildings.

But unsatisfactory as much of nineteenth-century architecture may seem

Administration Building of S.C. Johnson & Son, Inc., Racine, Wisconsin, lobby.
(Photograph, courtesy S.C. Johnson & Son, Inc.)

The Wainwright Building, St. Louis. (Photograph, Bill Hedrich, Hedrich-Blessing.)

today, it cleared the way for the modern movement. Downing was right in characterizing his time as an "experimental stage of architectural taste" in which the "people seem determined *to try everything*." Out of the restless experiments of the nineteenth century emerged a new architectural tradition. Central among the architectural legacies of the nineteenth century was the doctrine of functionalism, developed by the theoreticians of the Gothic Revival and stemming from the romantic veneration of nature. The loving regard for brick, stone, and wood shown in the buildings of Frank Lloyd Wright is better understood when it is remembered that the greatest of American artists regarded himself as the heir of Emerson and Whitman.

The dematerialization of form desired in religious structures by Downing and Eidlitz and given striking embodiment in Paxton's Crystal Palace anticipated the spatial feeling characteristic of such diverse modern creations as the Bauhaus of Walter Gropius [42] and the interior of Wright's Johnson Wax Administration Building. The Crystal Palace and related nineteenth-century structures rejected clearly defined spatial relations in an attempt to achieve an artificial infinity. Such monuments were the architectural equivalent of great works of romantic music and literature which rejected the limits of traditional form in the quest of a never wholly attainable ideal. Architectural indefiniteness became a goal in a period which found formal definitions uncomfortably confining.

Modern architecture has not returned to clear and logical space, but proceeding from the nineteenth-century feeling for demateriality, has developed a complex counterpoint based upon a certain amount of spatial ambiguity. Yet the modern movement has regained a sense of form generally lacking in romantic architecture. The reviving sense of geometric discipline appears in American architecture about 1885.[43] Its monuments are such diverse structures as Richardson's "four square" wholesale store for Marshall Field in Chicago and the Renaissance Palazzo which McKim, Mead and White designed for Henry Villard in New York. Unfortunately the new sense of order was almost immediately identified with the revival of Renaissance styles. This destroyed the free picturesque house architecture of the earlier eighties just as it was gaining the formal coherence necessary to make it completely satisfying esthetically. The Chicago school was also eclipsed, although Louis Sullivan's Wainwright building in St. Louis (1890–1891) had demonstrated that geometric order did not necessarily lead to revivalism.

Sullivan's pupil, Frank Lloyd Wright, absorbed from the academic revival what it had to teach of formal discipline and applied it to the picturesque

The Warren Hickox House, Kankakee, Ill., 1900, by Frank Lloyd Wright.
(Photograph, Fuermann. Chicago Architectural Photo Co.)

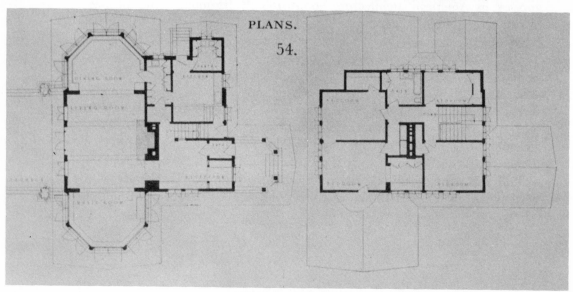

Plan of the Warren Hickox House.
(Courtesy Professor Henry-Russell Hitchcock)

The Ward Willitts House, Highland Park, Ill., 1902, by Frank Lloyd Wright.
(Photograph, Fuermann. Chicago Architectural Photo Co.)

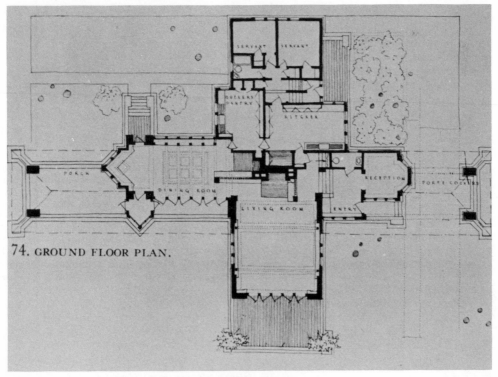

74. GROUND FLOOR PLAN.

Plan of the Ward Willitts House.
(Courtesy Professor Henry-Russell Hitchcock)

tradition of domestic architecture in a free and personal way.[44] Although the horizontal bands of windows in his prairie houses are broken with vertical strips reflecting the studs of the wooden frame, Wright valued plastic continuity of surface more than expression of the interior skeleton.[45] As a result of this sense of discipline, which was notably lacking in most picturesque wooden architecture, Wright's wall surfaces are able to mould form and space in a way which compares favorably with the great architectures of the past.

In both interior and exterior organization Wright's prairie houses represent an ordering of the patterns of nineteenth century-wooden architecture. His favorite L and cruciform plans of interpenetrating spatial volumes are further developments of the free spatial composition of the shingle style of the eighties. The free asymmetrical exterior massing of the picturesque tradition is also disciplined in the prairie houses. Wright's insistence on plastic continuity of surface enabled him to preserve esthetic coherence amid a complex interplay of solids and voids, vertical accents and broadly projecting eaves which serve to draw exterior space within the mass of the house much as had the porches of the earlier picturesque styles. Wright was unique among the major twentieth century architects in the extent of his debt to the picturesque tradition, but modern architecture as a whole is much more dependent upon nineteenth-century precedents than has been generally recognized. Few of the creative achievements of the twentieth century are conceivable apart from the picturesque revolt against static, symmetrical design and the romantic insistence that a building express its purpose and the means and materials of its construction.

Notes

1. *Democracy in America*, II, 48.
2. A contemporary attributed the proportions and ornaments of Greek and "other southern" architecture to an imitation of the palm tree and suggested that "we in the north introduce the proportions of the pine into our architecture, and ornament it with various natural productions peculiar to these latitudes. It would establish a national architecture, and be more appropriate and equally beautiful. The trunk of the pine might serve for the proportions of the shafts of the column, and the whole might be crowned by imitations of the staple productions of this country—the corn, the cotton, and the tobacco"—"Hints to American Architects," *The National Register,* vol. II, no. 14, 209. The belief that the palm tree provided the model for the classical columns and that northern architecture should be based on the pine is taken from Jacques H. Bernardin de Saint Pierre's *Harmonies of Nature* (London, 1815), I, 68–70, 87–90.

3. Letter to James Madison, September 20, 1785, *The Papers of Thomas Jefferson*, VIII, 462.

4. Notable among the critics of the Greek revival was Arthur D. Gilman. He wrote that "doric and plate glass have a natural antipathy" and argued that classical edifices "belong to another climate; they are the legitimate offspring of a remote age, an antagonistic religion, an obsolete form of government, and a widely different state of society from our own. With us they have no concern." "Architecture in the United States," *North American Review*, vol. LVIII, no. 123 (1844), 450, 453.

5. "New York Daguerreotyped," vol. I, no. 2 (1853), 132.

6. "Self-Reliance," in *Essays, First Series* (Standard Library Edition) (Boston and New York, n.d.), 81.

7. 3rd Series, vol. II, 246–249.

8. *Ibid.*, 247–249.

9. Vol. III, no. 4, 115; signed "R".

10. "A Few Words on Our Progress in Building," in *Rural Essays*, 215–216. Downing was quite willing to make concessions to the demand for houses with associational values. "Placing national feeling and national taste above all others, we will not," he wrote, "however, shut our eyes to the fact . . . that in every age and country are born some persons who belong rather to the past than the present. . . . It is not for these men, who love the past . . . to understand and appreciate the value of an architecture significant of the present time. And it is, therefore, for such as they to build houses in styles that recall the past"— *The Architecture of Country Houses*, 265. In another place Downing, believing that "individual habits and hereditary descent, when they are sufficiently marked may give a certain fitness to a given style of architecture," advocated houses in a Dutch style for old Dutch families—"Hints to Persons about Building in the Country," *loc. cit.*, xvii, n.

11. *Homes for the People*, 5, 23.

12. "Architecture in the United States," *loc. cit.*, 454–455, 463–469.

13. *Hints on Public Architecture*, 8, 65, 67.

14. From the notes of Richard M. Hunt printed in *The Crayon*, vol. V, no. 7 (1858), 200. On Lienau see Ellen W. Kramer, "Detlef Lienau," *Journal of the Society of Architectural Historians*, vol. XIV, no. 7 (1955), 218–225.

15. Wright's *Autobiography* (New York: Duell, Sloan & Pearce, 1943), 75.

16. "House Building in America," vol. X, no. 55 (1857), 109–111.

17. "Criticism in Search of Beauty," *A Memorial of Horatio Greenough*, 164.

18. "American Architecture," *A Memorial of Horatio Greenough*, 118.

19. Cf. *The Journals of Ralph Waldo Emerson*, VII, 333; *Excursions in Italy*, 33; *Notions of the Americans*, II, 115.

20. "Aesthetics at Washington," *A Memorial of Horatio Greenough*, 78; "American Architecture," *loc. cit.*, 118.

21. "Structure and Organization," *A Memorial of Horatio Greenough*, 173.

22. "American Architecture," *loc. cit.*, 125.

23. "Structure and Organization," *loc. cit.*, 182.

24. *Ibid.* Greenough's influence is shown in a series of articles "New York Daguerreotyped" in *Putnam's Magazine* (1853–54).

25. *Cottage Residences*, 53. Verandahs were introduced to England from the East by returning Anglo-Indians, Hitchcock, *Early Victorian Architecture in Britain*, 27.

26. Cf. *The Shingle Style*, especially 54–55, 63–64, 88.

27. Cf. Sigfried Giedion, *Space, Time and Architecture* (Cambridge: Harvard University Press, 1941), 105–107.

28. Letter of March 24, 1789, to Joseph Willard, *The Papers of Thomas Jefferson*, XIV, 698. Jefferson previously had corresponded with Paine about his bridge. Cf. Letter to Paine, December 23, 1788, XIV, 372–377.

29. *The Practical Builders' Assistant*, I, 104. The first edition of this book was published in Philadelphia in 1818 with the title, *The Builder's Assistant*.

30. *An Improved and Enlarged Edition of Biddle's Young Carpenter's Assistant* (Philadelphia, 1858), 45. Haviland's edition of this book was first published in 1837.

31. The lowest story was more substantial than Hatfield's but the upper four stories were cast from Hatfield's patterns. The best account of Bogardus's commercial architecture is Turpin C. Bannister, "Bogardus Revisited; Part I: The Iron Fronts," *Journal of the Society of Architectural Historians,* vol. XV, no. 4 (1956), 12–22.

32. *Cast Iron Buildings* (New York, 1856), 14.

33. *The Practical Builders' Assistant,* 104.

34. *Hints on Public Architecture,* 2.

35. *Eleven Weeks in Europe* (Boston, 1852), 286–287.

36. "Architecture," vol. III, no. 7, 214–215.

37. Giedion relates the Crystal Palace to the dematerialized late landscapes of Turner and cites a description of the building by Lothar Bucher which is certainly related to the conception of the Gothic held by Downing and Eidlitz—*op. cit.,* 188–190. Lothar described the interior as made up of "a delicate network of lines without any clue by means of which we might judge their distance from the eye or the real size. The side walls are too far apart to be embraced in a single glance. Instead of moving from the wall at one end to that at the other, the eye sweeps along an unending perspective which fades into the horizon. We cannot tell if this structure towers a hundred or a thousand feet above us, or whether the roof is a flat platform or is built up from a succession of ridges for there is no play of shadows to enable our optic nerves to gauge the measurements.

"If we let our gaze travel downward it encounters the blue-painted lattice girders. At first these occur only at wide intervals; then they range closer and closer together until they are interrupted by a dazzling band of light—the transept—which dissolves into a distant background where all materiality is blended into the atmosphere."

38. *Glances at Europe* (New York, 1851), 19.

39. "Our Crystal Palace," vol. II, no. 8 (1853), 121–122.

40. "Cast Iron in Decorative Architecture," *loc. cit.,* 15–20.

41. Thomas E. Tallmadge, *The Story of Architecture in America* (New York, 1927), chapter heading.

42. Giedion who related Paxton's work to that of Turner associated the spatial feeling embodied in the Bauhaus with that of cubist painting. In the Bauhaus "there is the hovering, vertical grouping of planes which satisfies our feeling for a relational space, and there is the extensive transparency that permits interior and exterior to be seen simultaneously, *en face* and *en profile,* like Picasso's 'L'Arlesienne' of 1911–12; variety of levels of reference, of points of reference and simultaneity—the conception of space-time, in short." *Op. cit.,* 402.

43. Vincent Scully traces this development in domestic architecture, *The Shingle Style,* 98, 113, 121, and ch. VIII.

44. Henry-Russell Hitchcock, "Frank Llloyd Wright and the Academic Tradition of the Early Eighteen-Nineties," *Journal of the Warburg and Courtauld Institutes,* VII (1944), 46–63.

45. Scully, *op. cit.,* 150, 160–161.

Index

Abbotsford, Selkirkshire, 84
Adam, Robert, 14, 21, 34
Adam, William, 14
Adams, Henry, 157
Adams, John, 115
Addison, Joseph, 31, 53
The Alhambra, 39
Alison, Archibald, 34–36
Allen, Lewis F., 60, 66
Allston, Washington, 86
American Institute of Architects, 98, 124, 155
Andalusia, Andalusia, Pa., 27–28, 47
Annapolis, 74
Archeology, 34, 48
"The Architect's Dream" by Thomas Cole, 41
Aristotle, 18
Associationism, 34–36, 47, 158
Asymetrical Design, 67–70
The Atheneum, Boston, 74
The Atheneum, Philadelphia, 73–74
Athens, 43

Baalbek, 14
Baltimore, 21
Baltimore Cathedral (Catholic), 40
The Bank of Pennsylvania, Philadelphia, 46
Barlow, Joel, 138
Barnum, P.T., 124
Barry, Sir Charles, 74
The Bauhaus, Dessau, 161
Benjamin, Asher, 21, 35, 47–48, 118, 129

Biddle, Nicholas, 27, 46–47, 138
Bierstadt, Albert, 85
Bogardus, James, 148–149, 151
Bonaparte, Napoleon, 45–46
Boston, 74, 96, 115
Brady, Josiah, 40
Britton, John, 48
Brown, Capability (Lancelot), 53
Brunelleschi, Filippo, 34
Bryant, William Cullen, 54, 88, 100
Bulfinch, Charles, 21, 40
Bumpo, Natty, 85
Burke, Edmund, 31, 53, 85
Burlington, Richard Boyle, 3rd Earl of, 17, 39

Cabot, J. Elliott, 101
Cambridge Camden Society, 125, 127
Canterbury Cathedral, 90
The Capitol of the United States, 33, 46, 74
Caruthers, William Alexander, 84
Castlewood House, Llewellyn Park, West
    Orange, New Jersey, 72
Catherine II, Queen of Russia, 45
Catholicism, 40, 112, 115, 119, 121, 127–128
Caylus, Anne-Claude-Phillipe de Tubières
    Comte de, 34
Central Park, New York, 55
Chamberlain, N.H., 122
Chambers, Sir William, 39
Charles VII, King of Naples, 34
Charleston, 74, 115

167

Chartres Cathedral, 85, 93
Chicago Architecture, 147, 157, 161
Chinese revival architecture, 39
Chiswick House, London, 39
Choragic Monument of Lysicrates (The Lantern of Demosthenes), Athens, 39
Christ Church, Cambridge, Mass., 17
Christ Church, Hartford, 118
Christ Church, Philadelphia, 114
Church of the Ascension, New York, 126
Church of the Savior, Boston, 121–122
Cicero, Marcus Tullius, 43
Clarke, James Freeman, 92, 152
Clarke, Thomas C., 121–122
Clérisseau, Charles-Louis, 13, 18
Cole, Thomas, 41, 85
Coleridge, Samuel Taylor, 86
Cologne Cathedral, 92
Color in Architecture, 65–67
The Colosseum, 36, 38–39
Congregationalism, 119–123, 128
Cooper, James Fenimore, 31, 43, 45, 54, 65–66, 85, 143
Cortona, Pietro da (Pietro Barrattini), 77–78
Cox, Samuel S., 89
The Crystal Palace, London, 152–153, 155, 161
The Crystal Palace, New York, 152, 154

Dakin, James H., 96
Dana, Richard Henry, 88
Davis, Alexander Jackson, 40, 55, 67–70, 74, 84–85, 96
Descartes, René, 17
Dewey, Orville, 123
Doane House, Burlington, N.J., 64
Downing, Andrew Jackson, 35, 54–67, 70–71, 76, 96, 100, 108, 123–124, 128, 140–141, 143, 147, 161
Downton Castle, Herefordshire, 54
Dughet, Gaspar, 53, 60
Duncan and Sherman's Bank, New York, 152
Dwight, Theodore Jr., 119

Eastburn, Manton, 126
Eastern State Penitentiary, Philadelphia, 96
Egyptian revival architecture, 39–40
Eidlitz, Leopold, 124–125, 141–142, 161
Electricity Building, World's Columbian Exposition, Chicago, 157

Ely Cathedral, 85, 93
Emerson, Ralph Waldo, 54, 88–89, 99–102, 107, 139, 143, 151–152, 161
Emerson, William Ralph, 144–145
Episcopalianism, 112–115, 118–120, 125–128, 157
The Enlightenment, 31, 34, 158
Episcopal Theological Seminary, Cambridge, 157
The Erectheum, 46

Federal Hall, New York, 138
Field, M., 61
Florence, 36
Florence Cathedral, 93, 156
Fonthill Castle, Riverdale, N.Y., 27, 29
Forrest, Edwin, 27
Fowler, O.S., 100–101
Fox, Samuel M., 46
Franklin, Benjamin, 147
Functionalism, 46–47, 70–71, 96–102, 107–108, 141–143, 152, 155–157, 161

Garvan, Anthony, 43
Ghent, 152
Gibbs, James, 14
Gilman, Arthur D., 122, 139, 141
Gilmor, Robert, 84
Girard College, Philadelphia, 46–47
Glen Ellen, Towson, Md., 84
Goethe, Johann Wolfgang von, 92, 96–97
Gothic Architecture, 31, 43, 48, 85–87, 89–93, 97-98, 112–113, 115, 121–126, 129, 131, 142
Gothic novelists, 84
Gothic revival architecture, 27, 29–30, 35, 39–40, 43, 54, 60–63, 65, 68, 70, 77, 79–80, 84–85, 93–99, 112, 115, 118–134, 141–142
Grace Church, New York, 119–120
Greece, 14, 46
Greek architecture, 17, 21, 25, 27, 46, 86–87, 98, 121–124, 140, 143
Greek revival architecture, 21, 27–28, 30, 34, 35, 39–49, 60, 62, 71, 74, 122, 139
Greeley, Horace, 155
Greene, John Holden, 40
Greenough, Horatio, 44, 101–102, 107–108, 143
Gropius, Walter, 161

Hallam, Robert A., 126–127

Harper and Brothers Building, New York, 148–149
Harrison, Peter, 17
Hart, J. Coleman, 122
Haskell, Llewellyn, 70
Haviland, John, 40, 55, 96, 147–148, 151
Hawthorne, Nathaniel, 87, 93
Hawthorne, Mrs. Nathaniel, 36, 39, 87, 93
The Hephaisteron, Athens, 27
Herder, Johann Gottfried von, 142
Hickox House, Kankakee, Ill., 162
Hills, Chester, 71
Hitchcock, Henry-Russell, 126
Hobart, Bishop John Henry, 118
Hone, Philip, 36, 119
Hopkins, Bishop John Henry, 89, 118–119, 123–124
House of Representatives, Washington, D.C., 33
Hume, David, 21
Hunt, Richard Morris, 98

Iranistan, Bridgeport, 124
Iron Construction, 147–157
Irving, Washington, 39, 51
Italian villas, 40, 60–62, 64–65, 69–71, 96

Jackson, Andrew, 40, 42
James I, King of England, 34
Jamestown, 112
Jarves, James Jackson, 36
The Jayne Building, Philadelphia, 94, 96
Jefferson, Thomas, 13–14, 17–18, 21, 31, 39–40, 43, 45–46, 54, 138, 147, 158
Johnson Administration Building, Racine, Wisc., 159, 161

Kennedy, John Pendleton, 84
Kent, William, 39
Kew Gardens, Surry, 39
Kimball, Fiske, 39
Kingscote, Newport, 77, 79–80
King's College Chapel, Cambridge, 30
Kirk, Edward N., 121–123
Knight, Richard Payne, 35, 53–55, 71

Labrouste, Henri, 141
Lafever, Minard, 35, 40, 71
Landscape gardens, 39, 53–55, 60

Landscape painting, 53–54, 60, 66
The Lantern of Demosthenes (Choragic Monument of Lysicrates), Athens, 39
Latrobe, Benjamin Henry, 21, 40, 43, 46–47, 54, 70, 138
Lee, Robert E., 40
L'Enfant, Pierre Charles, 22, 138
Lewis, Monk, 84
Lichfield Cathedral, 87
Lienau, Detlef, 141
Lincoln Cathedral, 93
Llewellyn Park, West Orange, New Jersey, 70, 74
Locke, John, 18, 21
London, 112
Longinus, 31
Long, Robert Cary, Jr., 140
Lorrain, Claude, 53–54, 60
Ludwig I, King of Bavaria, 46
Lyndhurst, Tarrytown, N.Y., 85

Madison, James, 13, 138
Maison Carrée, Nimes, 13–14, 17–19, 31, 138
Marshall Field wholesale store, Chicago, 161
McIntire, Samuel, 20–21
McKim, Mead and White, 161
Meason, G.L., 54
The Medici-Riccardi Palace, 36–37
Meeks, C.L.V., 75
Memorial Hall, Harvard, 155
Milan Cathedral, 89, 91–92, 115
Mills, Robert, 21
Mohammedan revival architecture, 39–40
Monticello, 39, 43, 54
Morris House, Philadelphia, 21–22
Morse, Samuel F.B., 33, 115
Morven, Princeton, N.J., 54
Mount Airy, Richmond County, Va., 14–15, 17–18
Mount Vernon, 54

Nationalism, 137–143
New Haven, 118
New Orleans, 21
Newport, 77, 79
Newport Parish Church (St. Luke's) Smithfield, Va., 112–113
Newton, Sir Isaac, 17–18, 21
New York City, 27, 96, 119, 139

New York City Hall, 23, 25
New York Ecclesiological Society, 125–128
New York University, 95–96
Nîmes, 13, 45
Notman, John, 55, 64, 73–74

Oak Hill, Peabody, Mass., 20
The Old Public Library, Boston, 74
Old Ship Meeting House, Hingham, Mass.,
    115–117
Old South Meeting House, Boston, 115
Olmsted, Frederick Law, 55
Organic theories of form, 87–93, 96–102, 107–
    108
Owen, Robert Dale, 93, 102–104, 141, 151

Paine, Tom, 147
Palladian Architecture, 14–15, 17, 18, 21, 25,
    35, 39, 53–54, 62
Palladio, Andrea, 14, 35
Palmyra, 14
The Pantheon, 31–32, 39, 46–47, 86
The Parthenon, 30, 45, 143
Paxton, Sir Joseph, 152–153, 155, 161
Penn Mutual Life Insurance Building, Phila-
    delphia, 148
Philadelphia, 21, 46, 96, 115
Phillips, Willard, 88
Picturesque architecture, 51–80, 158
Pliny, the younger, 40, 43
Poe, Edgar Allan, 39
Polk, James K., 40
Pope, Alexander, 53–54, 89
Poussin, Nicholas, 53, 60
Price, Sir Uvedale, 53, 55, 62, 66
Protestantism, 40, 43, 112–134
Pugin, Augustus, 48
Pugin, Augustus Northmore Welby, 97, 100,
    122, 127–129

Radcliffe, Ann, 84
Ranlett, William H., 71
Reed, Sampson, 88
Randolph, Edmund, 13
Rathbone House, Albany, N.Y., 63
Renaissance architecture, 36
Renaissance revival architecture, 74–75, 96,
    141, 148–151
Renwick, James, Sr., 96

Renwick, James, 85, 119–120, 128
Repton, Humphry, 53, 55
Revett, Nicholas, 34, 46, 48
Reynolds, Sir Joshua, 17, 66
Richardson, Henry Hobson, 161
Rickman, Thomas, 48
Rockaway, New York, 36
Rogers, Isaiah, 40
Roman architecture, 17–18, 25, 45–46, 138
Romanesque revival architecture, 40, 85, 141
Rome, 14
Rosa, Salvator, 53
Rouen Cathedral, 85, 152
The Royal Academy, 18
Ruskin, John, 75, 92–93, 97–98, 128

St. George's Church, Stuyvesant Square, New
    York, 127
St. James Church, New London, 126
St. Luke's Church (Newport Parish Church),
    Smithfield, Va., 112–113
St. Paul's Church, Buffalo, 129, 132–134
St. Stephen's Church, Philadelphia, 118
Salem, Mass., 96
Sansovino, Jacapo, 75
Santa Maria della Pace, Rome, 77–78
Schelling, Friedrich Wilhelm Joseph von, 89,
    101
Schlegel, August Wilhelm, 86
Schlegel, Friedrich, 86, 92, 125
Scotch-Realism, 21
Scott, Geoffrey, 75
Scott, Sir Walter, 43, 84–85
Scully, Vincent J., 70, 108, 147
Second Bank of the United States, Philadel-
    phia, 24–25, 46
Sedgely, Philadelphia, 40
Shaftesbury, Anthony Ashley Cooper, 3rd Earl
    of, 53
Shakespeare, William, 86
Shaw, Edward, 97–98
The Shingle Style, 108, 144–147
Simms, William Gilmore, 85
Smith, Oliver P., 62
Smithsonian Institution, Washington, D.C., 74,
    85, 102–104
Society of Dilatanti, 34
Sophocles, 86
Springfield, Mass., City Hall, 85

Stevens, John Calvin, 146
Stockton, Richard, 54
Strasbourg Cathedral, 97
Strickland, William, 21, 25, 40, 47
Stuart, James, 34, 46, 48
The Sublime, 30–31
Sullivan, Louis H., 107, 141, 157, 160–161
The Sun Building, Baltimore, 148, 150–151
Sunnyside, Tarrytown, N.Y., 51–52
Swedenborg, Emanuel, 88
Syracuse Court House, 85

Tait, John R., 92
Tappan, Henry P., 121
Taylor, Bayard, 92
Tessé, Comtesse de, 45
Thomson, John W., 151
Thoreau, Henry David, 88, 101–102
Tocqueville, Alexis de, 27, 137
Town, Ithiel, 40, 96
Trinity Church, Boston, 118–119
Trinity Church, New York, 85, 126, 129–130
Trinity Church, Pittsburgh, 118
Tuthill, Mrs. L.C., 80
Twain, Mark, 157
Twickenham, Middlesex, 53–54

Unitarianism, 121–123
Upjohn, Richard, 77, 79–80, 85, 126–134

Van Brunt, Henry, 98, 155–156
Varro, Marcus Terentius, 43
Vaux, Calvert, 55, 60, 66, 75–77
Villard House, New York, 161

Viollet-le-Duc, Eugène Emmanuel, 141
Virginia State Capitol, Richmond, 13, 16–18, 21, 138
Vitruvius Pollio, 18, 98

Wallace, Horace B., 93, 98
Walter, Thomas U., 46–47, 74
Warburton, Bishop William, 88
Ward, Samuel G., 98–99
Ware, William R., 157
Wainwright Building, St. Louis, 160–161
Washington, D.C., 21, 40, 43, 55, 74
Washington, George, 43, 44, 54
George Washington, by Horatio Greenough, 44
Waterman, Thomas T., 14
Webster, Noah, 138–139
Westminster Abbey, 86, 92
Wheeler, Gervase, 60, 70–71, 100, 108, 128, 141, 147
Whitman, Walt, 139, 161
Willard, Solomon, 40
Williamsburg, Virginia, 74, 112
Willis, Frank, 128
Willitts House, Highland Park, Ill., 163
Winchester Cathedral, 131
Wölfflin, Heinrich, 75
Wood, Robert, 34
Worcester Railroad Station, 157
Wordsworth, William, 66, 88, 92, 97, 100, 151
Wren, Sir Christopher, 112, 115, 118
Wright, Frank Lloyd, 107, 142, 159, 161–164

York Minster, 86, 89